THE PATH OF THE HEART

THE PATH OF THE HEART

BY

WILLIAM AND JOY JENKINS

ISBN: 1-58820-040-X

Library of Congress Control Number: 2002102662

Printed in the United States of America
Bloomington, IN

1stBooks - rev. 6/15/02

To
Jodie Anne and Jennifer Lee Wertheim
from both of us
with love always

Acknowledgements

We are grateful to God for what we have learned and to Jesus for the great gift of being able to stay together, despite the circumstances of our lives. We are also grateful for the opportunity to share our story, that it might help others, who want to achieve of the path of the heart.

We want to thank our children, Jodie and Jennifer Wertheim, for loving and supporting us unconditionally through our changes. We also want to thank Jane Roosevelt, for always being there as our best friend and constant companion. We want to thank the many guides who cared for us on our journey, especially Mary Claire, Damien and Victor. But most of all, we want to thank Matheu, for whom there are no words to express our love and gratitude.

This is a true story

Prologue, Song of The Children

Against my will, I was born. Out of the warmth into the chill, I was excommunicated from the safety of my cathedral, where I felt connected to something greater than myself, struggling to survive, to even breathe on my own.

In that moment I lost everything. I felt pain for the first time. I was abandoned and alone. When they cut that cord, my last hope, I knew there was no way back, no way to recapture that feeling of belonging. In that instant, my connection with everything and everyone was destroyed. I not only lost my mother, who was my protector, but the essence of God himself dissolved to a lesser world. The knowingness evaporated into nothingness and through my tears I lost all meaning of life and love. I was born a coward for I was afraid.

And so my search began for the sanctity of that lost world. I knew that if I sought long enough and hard enough I would find it.

Now, some parents help, they hold you and stroke you, and almost convince you that you are still a part of them. Some don't. They neglect you and bruise you, and leave you hanging in an emotional abyss, making everything worse than it already is.

First, they send you to school to learn the truth, which rings untrue in the bell tower of your heart. Then, they send you to church, and tell you to pray to some invisible God, repeating some magic words, as if they are trying to appease him. But in your heart of hearts you know that you won't find him there, because from the beginning he was always around and within you, in silence and in glory and in peace, filling that emptiness with no struggle at all. So you do what they say, and you leave the church empty. But they don't seem to understand as they recite their catechism, looking for him in empty words that are always changing.

The years continue to pass, and you keep searching despite the difficulties, for something is driving you forward. You grow up despite everything, bodies stretching out, hearts holding more things in, not flowing anymore, but stumbling, not pure, but polluted, then nature takes over, and in the end you survive in this jungle in an animalistic way.

In your heart you are empty and you know that something is very wrong. You don't quite seem attached to anything or anyone, and you feel like you are floating out there like a bird without a perch, or a ship without a shore. And you keep looking for your immutable faith.

Nothing seems to work, everything is constantly changing, people come and go, accidents happen, you move around in circles as others are born and others die. The cycle continues endlessly.

At times you experiment with substitutes to fill that need to be connected to something. You form friendships, you maintain relationships, you even get married, but find they weren't it after all. You are afraid your children will inherit your emptiness.

Sometimes you are soothed and fed, but still unsatisfied. Because somewhere on some level you know that something is missing. Your appetite is being fed, but your hunger remains because it's all junk food.

Then one day, when you have almost given up hope, and both your heart and your soul are exhausted beyond human resources; when you have stopped running in circles looking at everyone and everything, wondering what it is that you need to find; when you are sitting alone in the stillness of defeat ready to give up, rather than to go on hopeless and conquered by this world which has fed your surface, but left your soul starving; whether by chance or by design, you look inside yourself instead of outside, and in an instant you find Him there.

What suprises you even more is that you can see Him, hear Him, and feel Him, within you and without you, his acknowledgement surrounding you, just as he did before you were born. And somewhere inside you a distant memory reawakens, and you are at peace for the first time in your life, for you have finally come home.

All false lovers fade in the face of true love. In that shining moment of unconditional love, everything falls into place, and you are reborn again. You were born a coward, but now you are a hero, for God is real and you have found Him.

Song of The Channel

In our time, there exists a place called Pennsylvania. Pennsylvania is a state that is part of a greater whole called the United States, which is yet part of a greater unity called the Earth, which is just a pinprick in the sky of what is called the Universe. Nobody really knew what lay beyond the universe, for it was beyond what man's eye could see, but some men had developed a keenness of vision called intuition, and had sensed worlds of multidimensional realities leading out to infinity.

Nobody really knew how many layers there were. People moved about like ants, some going about their everyday lives, noses to the perpetual grindstones; while others were exploring the universe in their minds, heads in the stars, expanding the vision of humanity. Some lived in the moment, some in the past, and some dreamed dreams of the future. The world was diverse in its creation. There were ordinary men of ordinary vision, great men of heroic vision, philosophers, poets, pimps and even kings. But all were equal in their expectations of finding peace within themselves and their place in the universe.

On a farm called Meadowbrook, where the flowing fields seemed like bottomless green oceans beached by massive pines, there lived a girl who struggled to find her place in the scheme of things. Upon her birth she was given a very happy name. "Let's call her Joy," so happy were they to have a child of their own. I was that girl from Pennsylvania.

All fairy tales grow more complicated upon closer scrutiny. Life was ideallic on the outside. But everyone knows the outer world is nothing but an illusion created by man for all the world to see and foolishly believe.

"She is so stupid," my mother used to say, amongst other things, then go about her business of being a stern educator, while smoke poured from her eyes, nose and mouth like a ferocious dragon. My father, soft and gentle, melted into the background amidst the fire that was his wife. He taught me to tie my shoes so I wouldn't be punished, but he was no knight, for he

1

could not slay the dragon. I knew then I was not a beautiful princess, for they kept me hidden and alone, doing their bidding.

Many times, I would see spirit when I was little. But I was born afraid and lived afraid of the beautiful silken visions of men and women that would smile gently at me and offer me solace. I would hide under my bed until the visions passed. When I told my mother about them, I was sent to a convent school, where the nuns kept me away from the other children playing in the playground. I sat alone behind convent walls until my mother came to take me home, listening as they revealed to her that I was truly hopeless and crazy, which only increased the puinshment, and the cruelty of her love.

As I grew up, I was surrounded by natural wealth, and I spent many hours dreaming in both the fields and the forests, away from the house where I was a prisoner. My parents were both hard working people who, despite their shortcomings, tried to provide the very best materially for me, their only hopeless child. The home I lived in was very beautiful, and though I was always lonely, I didn't have to worry much about money, as they had provided for that. My struggle to survive did not come from the outside, but from within, for I felt very much alone, and in spite of all that I had, I felt I had nothing.

I felt worthless, and everytime I looked in a mirror, despite what my eyes told me, I saw nothing. Now everyone knows that you can't always believe in what you see, for true wealth and beauty comes from within where it can not be seen by the naked eye. No matter where you live, or, what you have, life can only be beautiful if you believe in yourself. I did not believe in myself.

As time went on, I took care of my parents in a loving way, wondering if I would ever fill that emptiness inside, and feel worthwhile in this world. So I worked hard at earning that importance by the things I did for them, yet, I still did nothing for myself, for I knew I was nothing.

Time is like a river that never stops flowing, its current sweeping you along from places that are familiar, to other places that are strange and foreign to your nature, almost against your will. On my journey I went to school, I went to church, I made

2

many friends, and had many relationships. But everywhere the river took me, I was left wanting, for I was unable to fill that need.

In my twenties I got married to a shadow of a man to have some company, but it didn't last long, for there was still something missing. The closest I came to love and fulfillment was with my children. They were both beautiful and bright, and I loved them deeply. And they, in the innocence of all children loved me back. That was my first experience with unconditional love, for in them I saw the perfection of all things, and they believed in me.

Jodie and Jennifer, the two beautiful girls I had were very much like myself. And the three of us became almost as one islet in the river of time. I always let them know how much I loved them. But somewhere deep inside of me, I knew that my children must grow up and be allowed to begin their own search for themselves. I didn't want to hold on to them, and deny them their truth, like my mother before me. So I felt even worse, for I wanted to leave them a legacy of faith, instead of the doubt and fear that I still found myself constantly in.

So life went on humming, the sun rose every morning only to be replaced by the moon at night, and the earth was full of many footsteps that led in many diverse directions, but never seemed to lead to anywhere special.

Sometimes we all went to shopping malls, and I would buy them the many trinkets that girls are so fond of. Sometimes I bought something for me. "If I buy this," I thought, "I'll feel better about myself." But the blissful feeling would always wear off in time, and I would be left again feeling bleak and lonely, insecure in my beliefs with nothing to hold onto, hungry for something more to fill that emptiness inside.

Sometimes we would go to the movies, which would take us out of ourselves, carrying us to a different time and place, where for a few fleeting moments, all the pieces would seem to fit, and we, like the characters in the movies, would find happiness. But when the movie ended and the theatre lights came back on, we were still ourselves again, searching for something indefinable.

We tried fortune tellers, that rare breed that pretended to know something. But mostly what they knew was trivial and unimportant, like who would cross your path and who wouldn't. There was never anything of substance, and I was reminded of stick figures with no souls, for they only skimmed the surface, and avoided the depth. Fortune tellers, and their brethren psychics don't swim in deep water, and I was left hungry, for I had many questions still unanswered for myself and my children, as to the meaning of life, and where was my soul. But the soothsayers pretended not to understand, and tried to cover their ignorance by feeding me garbage for my personality, while they starved my soul.

So Pennsylvania continued to be part of the greater whole called the United States, and the earth rotated on its axis; while the sun and the moon alternated their duty in the sky, and life went on spinning in endless circles, constantly moving, but going nowhere. And I went on spinning with it.

Time seemed like a loom to me, which continued to weave the same pattern over and over, and I felt like a woman who had been wearing the same dress for years, a shipwreck survivor, without passage to anywhere, not knowing if I would ever be rescued. Even though things appeared to change at times, I recognized they were still the same. In quiet desperation, I turned more and more inward. And one day, while taking a simple bath, I unlocked the door to what I had been looking for quite innocently.

I felt as if I were floating in a lake that had no bottom, and though I couldn't swim, I wasn't afraid, for the water itself held me up with tranquil arms, allowing me to forget about everything for those few splendid moments in time. Within the cool darkness of the water, there was light surrounding me and filling me with its warmth.

Then, my arm touched the barrier of the side of the tub and I remembered who I was. The timelessness faded, as I touched bottom to become once again of this world. Random thoughts started to weigh me down, as I struggled to let go of time and space once more, to leave the circumference of the tub in my mind, and to return to that timeless and limitless environment of

4

that ocean. But stupid things held me back and led me astray, until I finally gave in to mortality and rose shivering into the morning air, panting and dripping wet, as I lay in an old robe on the bathroom floor.

This became a normal part of my routine. Brief moments out of time, where the peacefulness led me to places known only by the human spirit, then to be forced to return to time, to the place of the body that only knew imprisonment of that same spirit. My time in the bath was my only freedom from bondage, and little did I know I had subconsciously learned something of great importance, for my experience was very personal.

I had received without asking, the answer to an essential question. That a bathtub could truly become an ocean in the human mind, showed that we as physical people create our own barriers in our physical bodies. Our souls have no limits, and when we remember who we truly are, these barriers are lifted, for we are what we choose ourselves to be, ultimately, creating our own reality.

Yet, I didn't think it through in so many words, but just knew something was happening to me, and I felt changed for the better in some way.

So I began taking a lot of baths, drawn to that weightless feeling where all time and space left me, and there was no bottom. Nothing could touch me there, and I felt as if I were floating in the womb of the universe itself.

After awhile I felt myself growing stronger, as my thoughts became less cluttered and more focused. I began to face my life with a clarity of mind and an energized body, as I connected with a greater energy outside my own, which I could not identify, but which sustained and fed my starving soul.

One day, I decided to try to expand this experience by attempting it on dry land. So like a sailor coming from the sea, I rose from the tub and sat in a chair seeking eternity.

My tenseness slowly eased, as I began by taking many deep breaths, forcing air as if I were suffocating, until gradually my breathing became deeper and slower, and I began to feel lighter within myself. Then I began to flow with the current, and I felt as I had in the water, weightless, and once again buoyant and bobbing like a cork. The tide took me out and all time vanished, as I became one with a force greater than my own.

I began a journey that day, and though I didn't know it, my life would never be the same again. I felt as if there were no boundaries, no time or space, as my physical body vanished. My mind became empty, but focused and keenly aware of the vast beyond. Like an astronaut in a rocket ship, the chair I was in, Pennsylvania, and the planet Earth, faded from view, as I was swept away in the Universe.

How much time passed, I don't know, but I found I could still see, even though my eyes were closed. In fact, my vision was clearer than ever before. Like an eagle I began to see something in my clear mind's eye. It was a person, far off in the distance. From that distance, it seemed very small. I sat there mesmerized by that figure, watching as it moved slowly towards me, gaining in size as it came closer.

Its features were indistinguishable. It grew larger, until it stood right before me, and I could see its human form. It was a man, and he seemed very tall standing directly in front of the smallness that was me in the chair.

He was illuminated by a strange light, and I could feel the electricity of his being around me, making my hair stand on end. He stood in quiet majestic strength before me, larger than life itself. I did not feel threatened, but uncomfortable, for I began to feel very hot, surrounded by the sun of his prescence.

"Are you of God," I whispered in my mind, in total awe, not knowing what else to say, for be it God or Devil, he was there, and I wanted to communicate. He obviously understood my question, for he nodded his head in confirmation of that which I had already known in my heart, for the love I had felt from him could only come from God, and everyone knows the geiger counter of the heart is never wrong, when truly heard and listened to.

His garb was strange. He wore a cloak and a hood, which appeared to be the habit of a monk of ancient times. Just within the shadow of his hood, one could see an angular face, piercing blue eyes, and tendrils of curly black hair, peeping out around the corners of his forehead. There was a radiance around him as he patiently stood there watching me. I began to feel weak from the heat, for it was as if a piece of the sun had broken off and stood before me, warming, yet burning me at the same time. It was almost too much for me, for my physical body was only capable of sustaining the force of so much energy, and he obviously had more than a human could bear.

We both looked at each other for quite some time. He seemed to be searching my soul with his penetrating eyes, yet I wasn't offended, or afraid, for I was doing the same thing. I felt somehow comforted by his attention, he, in his dark grey habit and hood, and me, in my flowing, pale nightdress. We were quite obviously from different worlds, but seemed somehow linked.

Then the impossible happened. As I sat there, this huge monk lifted his arm, his sleeve streaming down to his wrist, and thrust it forward into my chest up to his elbow. His arm went right through me, for it was made of energy, not of flesh, and he held it in my chest. I felt searing pain in my heart, as if I were going to have a heart attack. My chest heaved, as my heart pounded, accelerating its beat, until I felt I was going to explode. At that point, he quickly removed his arm from me, and it was then that I knew for sure he didn't want to hurt me.

I rested for a few moments, chest still aching, as my heartbeat returned to normal. Then he stuck his arm in me again. But the same thing happened. My chest ached furiously, my heart pounded against my ribcage, and I had trouble breathing. He quickly withdrew his arm again. I knew now that his vibration was much higher than my own, and my physical body was ill equipped to carry such a current.

For a moment we both rested, waiting for my system to quiet. My heartbeat returned to normal, and the sharpness of the pain slowly died away. Then I slowly faced him again, displaying all of my courage, and like an adventurer on a quest, I welcomed his arm again, pushing me to the brink of physical death. He withdrew his arm just at the right moment.

This ritual went on for days. Each day I would return to my chair, and he would always come. It was during this time that we made a silent commitment to each other. I vowed to hold his energy within mine, as he seemed determined to raise my vibration, and to be held by me.

After about a week, I was able to accept him without too much discomfort. Then one day he came and without warning, simply sat down, in my body in the chair. The shock jolted me, and for a moment as our two beings merged, I didn't know who I was. I had trouble breathing as his energy swelled mine to gigantic proportions. But I had learned from practice that by taking slow deep breaths I could withstand more. I felt as big as a mountain, holding his soul, as well as my own in my small body, and I felt super human, for I had connected both worlds.

It was a magnificent feeling of both power and vulnerability as our energies merged for the first time. I was myself, yet more. His head was within my head, his hood graced us both, his arms were within my arms, his strong masculine torso was in my feminine one, and his flowing robe flowed down my slender legs. It was like holding and being held at the same time.

Days went by, and we continued to meet until it became quite comfortable for me to hold him in my body, and he would slip in as easily as my hand into a glove. I got used to the feeling of being more than myself, and felt strongly connected to him even when I was doing other things. I sensed his prescence around me all the time.

It was like any other day, yet I was quite unprepared for what would happen next. I began by deep breathing, and soon found this world slipping away. He was there as always, this imposing figure, slipping, now quite gently and easily into my being. We sat quietly for a time, but then I heard something I had never heard before. It was a voice and it was not my own. My own inner voice was a soprano, which raced along at staccato pace. What I heard quite clearly, was a baritone, speaking slowly and deliberately, that resounded of great strength and was very different from my own inner voice, which worried and clucked like a chicken in my mind. The voice spoke over my own, and the sound of it brought peace to my heart and a sense of security that I had never felt before.

I was like a little child hearing its mother's voice for the first time. He said quite calmly, and with a sense of fun, "My name is quite long, and you will never get it right, so you can call me Matheu, it will be easier for you."

And so from that moment on I was never alone again. I had many friends in my life, but time had always changed them, or me, or our circumstance, and even those I had maintained long term relationships with couldn't quite understand my lonliness, or feel my pain.

But Matheu did in a way that was beyond mortal understanding. He not only knew me, the girl, but he knew my soul as well. He was always there for me, and we would spend hours every day discussing even the most trivial things.

He explained to me that he was my guide, and had always been since I was a small child. He told me that he would nurture me, so that I could grow and nurture others with Divine Love.

Now, most people will ask, "What are the secrets he unlocked for you in the universe?" They are hungry for knowledge, and for understanding, as to their place in the scheme of things. But mostly what they are hungry for is love, though they don't know it. It is true that he taught me many things, but none more important than the love we shared.

He taught me how to pray, for God was his Father, as well as the Father of all mankind, and he taught me how to honor Him, and to emulate Him, in deed and in action. He taught me how to laugh, by telling me jokes and singing songs to me in many different languages. He taught me immutable faith and how to believe in myself.

Love was the tie that bound us together, and our faith in that love. I accepted him and he accepted me, and together we grew, as father and daughter, emulating by example Divine Love. All else was trivial compared with that love and that faith, for everyone knows faith and love are not an intellectual process, but one of the heart, that cannot be spoken, but must be experienced. They are the beginning and the ending from where all true knowledge comes, in full circle, in that same place and in that same spirit.

And so the years passed, and we grew together, the great guide, and the woman-child. He was patient and understanding, and would answer each and every question I had with wit and

9

wisdom. He became a parent to me, completing the process my own parents had abandoned so long ago for other things.

He prepared me for everyday life by bolstering my confidence in myself, and since he could clearly see both the future and the past, he expanded my vision of myself, those around me, and the universe itself. He was not only my teacher, but playmate as well, and he would pop into my body at unexpected times, and was quite physical with me, such as rubbing my neck when I was tired, patting me on the behind when I was cranky, and even driving my car home when I was upset.

He was my guide, but more than that, for he raised me in such a way that I began to grow into a confident adult and the person I was destined to be. And sometimes when I slept, he stood by my bed, and I would open my eyes to see him standing there, gazing down with love at the sleeping child within.

I loved him as I had never loved anyone before, and he loved me more than was humanly possible. Together we loved my children, and raised them, and soon my home was filled with the laughter and the love that only the prescence of an angel could bring.

My children came to know him through me, and they accepted him as a part of our family, with the same innocence that had blessed us with such a strong protector, for we had always known in our hearts that the truth of higher knowledge is only love. I knew it was a gift from God, and I felt beautiful, for the first time.

Time continued spinning, weaving us all together, but the pattern changed and as the moments became days, the threads began to shine with hope, and as the days became months, and finally years, the blanket of our lives became one of unconditional love.

Everything appeared the same on the outside, but distant friends and neighbors began to notice a change in me. I looked the same, but I didn't seem the same to them. My energy began to grow within me, as did my children's energy. Even though life itself still held many challenges, we met them with a very different outlook, which was one of faith, instead of despair. My children were remarkable, as they blended the best of Matheu's wisdom with that of their own, and they seemed wise beyond their young years, yet innocent and full of love and laughter.

"Matheu," they asked in desperation, "our hamster has run away. Can you find him?"

"Morning Sun and Fireball, my little ones, I am not a rodent specialist. I detect many rodents in this house. Perhaps the field mice are moving in. I am afraid that he has gone away. Sometimes in this life you must let go of things to allow better things to come along. Let him go on his way and know that you will find another pet to love, and that he will be safe on his journey in God's hands."

No question was too small, nor problem too big for the great guide when it came to the children, for they were the future of the universe itself, and a part of his heart.

Matheu and I spent more and more time together, sometimes in trance for more than half the day. We shared each other's worlds, and even when I wasn't in trance, he was there, popping in and out of my body as needed, or, just for fun. I learned from him what I should have learned in my childhood, but didn't, which was unconditional love. Everyone knows that without unconditional love one cannot grow in strength, but evolves in weakness and in fear. And so I passed that lesson and that love on to those around me, in both thought and deed.

I was not the same cellularly, for with my physical acceptance of him, my physical energy had changed and my body had chemically altered to hold the higher current that was required of it. I had been cellularly restructured and many nights I felt his invisible hands working on my chakras and my physical body to complete the task.

He taught me the healing arts and how to work with the healing light of God, sending it to those in need. The light itself was of great physical intensity, and through healing others, I learned to heal myself.

He taught me how to manifest the bounty of the universe as I needed it. He explained that there were no barriers, only those that man had created for himself, and that the universe was filled

11

with abundance, which was available to all for their highest good.

I was an apt pupil, a master at healing and at manifesting. Twice I manifested two thousand dollars in winnings playing a simple gambling game, to attend a healing seminar at Matheu's request, which cost exactly that much, and which the household budget did not contain.

I began to work more in healing others and those in need seemed drawn to my energy. But I never forgot my teachers, and to those who turned to me, I would tell them the story of Matheu, and of God, never taking credit for what I could see or do, for I knew all blessings came from God himself, and were passed along through the generations, as a legacy of love from Father to child.

Soon I began to expand my physical friendships, for I found others like myself. It was not unusual for me to have a conversation with Matheu, then to pick up the phone to speak with another channel, and to have Matheu continue our conversation through that other channel.

Each channel had their own guide, and we became a network of people helping each other, some with bodies, some without, supporting each other on our various paths. True channels were rare, but they exist, and they were very different from that breed known as psychics, who only see their own reflection, and cannot see your soul.

But, there was no guide like Matheu, for he seemed to move Heaven and Earth to protect me and my children, and he became a legend among his own kind.

We had an agreement that he would walk the path of my life with me. I could count on him. At times, other channels changed guides. Each guide served a purpose in an individual channel's life, and when that purpose was served and those lessons learned, another guide would come in to continue the lessons needed in that new area of spiritual growth. Each human channel's needs were different, and each guide was different, and would try to best serve the needs of the individual.

But Matheu seemed to have no boundaries in his service to God and mankind. He spoke many languages fluently, and taught me in Latin, Italian, and French. He also loved red wine, and would enter my body to experience the physical flavor of it.

He had a great sense of humor, and many times I would sit down to consult with him on what was of earth shattering importance to me, only to hear, "There was a young man from Brazil..."

He taught with every tool available to him, and he knew how to lighten my heart to knowledge. I grew without even knowing I was growing. Everyone knows that true knowledge is not taught, but lived, and we became the essence of spiritual growth, without thinking about it, in light, love and laughter.

At times he would bring other guides with him, until my house was filled with the energy of many teachers. I would experience them in the same physical way I had experienced him. Each had their own different physical energy, personality, wisdom and wit. I would listen to each and every one with the same love and respect that I had given him, for each had their own perception of life and had come to teach me. He would stand nearby, watching, proud that my vision was growing.

Like a doting father, he would introduce me to his guide colleagues and so I became very well known on the other side, as Matheu had among my own friends.

After awhile, I became more of those higher dimensions than of the physical plane, having removed those boundaries which only existed in my mind. I hoped that one day, like me, all mankind would finally be multidimensional as he was meant to be, united and a part of God.

Mary Claire was a wonderful guide that became a frequent visitor to my home. She was the guide of one of my friends, but would always come to check on one of "her children." Her soft and gentle energy was that of motherly love, which balanced out Matheu's masculine energy. She was very perceptive and spoke her truth in a soft and gentle voice, which soothed and calmed even the strongest of fears. She was a healer, and no hurt was too big or too small for her attention. Mary Claire was a nun in traditional dress, except for her shoes. She always wore comfortable, athletic shoes with laces.

Sometimes Doreena would come, with her hair in a bun and smelling of sweet water, talking you through the hardest lesson, like a professor patiently teaching calculus to a preschooler.

Grandfather was an Indian Chief of the Sioux nation, and proudly spoke of the ways of his people and their heritage. He was the family historian. Many nights he would lead the discussion on the past, incorporating those lessons into the present and finally into the future. He spoke of nature and planetary changes, and what would result from them.

Ashtar was not in spirit, but in physical body. He was an extraterrestrial from another galaxy with telepathic powers. He would join in on occasion, as he had with other channels. He had developed a broad reputation, contacting many earth friends with his mind. He was an intergalactic ambassador, teaching unity between all beings and uniting the galaxies themselves.

Adelaide had red hair and wore lilac perfume, which would fill the air. Clicking on high heels, her entrance would light up the room. She was known to impatience and quick action. Not wanting to talk anything through, she would get right to the point before the other guides could stop her. She could not tolerate injustice of any kind.

Twinkles was very different from the others. All of the guides had previously been in physical form. Twinkles had not, and was a cherub, without masculine or feminine energy. Made solely of light energy which had never been dimmed or restricted by the physical, Twinkles could dispell darkness simply by being there. The laughter of a cherub is contagious, their heart boundless, and all fear fled with the tinkling sound of a cherub's voice.

Then there was Damien, with his bulbous nose, who wore a feather in his old hat. There was no problem too great or too small, and he would patiently examine every angle, part rocket scientist, part medicine man, giving formulas for the solution to solving it. If a mountain needed to be moved, he knew how to move it, through whatever means necessary. He constantly roamed in his diverse energy, taking care of everyone along the way.

There were many others, whose energies graced my small room, too many to mention. But each in their own way brought with them faith in God, love of mankind, and an indomitable spirit to heal those who needed it. They were great teachers, and even greater friends, who had found in the limitless environment of the universe, a home away from home in Pennsylvania.

It was almost as if the universe had opened up, and hundreds of guides would just drop by, offering their advice, love and friendship, as fellow travelers on their journey to spiritual growth. My home became a portal, to both those in body and those out of body, and no one was turned away, for they were all brethren and God's children.

I welcomed them all, loving them with the open heart of a child, for they were not teachers to me, but friends and family. My house became vibrant with energy, a symphony of many voices, and Matheu was the conductor of it all.

Five years had passed, and one day Matheu gave me a new name. He explained that my personality in this lifetime was part of a greater soul, which extended without limit, through the many dimensions of reality to the Source.

My personality was only a single facet of that greater multifaceted soul, as souls send out small parts of themselves, never the entirety, to experience life in many different dimensions at the same time, in their pursuit of perfection. From that day on, I was acknowledged for who I truly was. I had earned the right to my soul name, through my hard work at becoming one with my soul. I was called Astarte, and they were proud of me. For the first time in my life, I felt proud of myself.

I continued my channeling, and much of it focused on helping the individual through the diagnosis of physical and emotional problems by reading their soul and its growth, to create a healthier individual and a happier life for them.

There were very special times when the archangels would appear, speaking not of earthbound things, but of the greater purpose of becoming one with God in universal love.

Michael, Haniel, Raphael, Uriel, and Gabriel all shared their wisdom with me, and would come unexpectedly and alone, to deliver their message. Their energy was much more powerful than the rest, and they didn't linger, but they left behind an even greater peace than I had ever known before.

Then one day He came. I had sat down to channel, and He was there in an instant. There was no effort or struggle, no forced connection.

His voice was as clear as a bell, and it vibrated through every part of my being. I knew Him before he spoke His name, for my heart identified Him. He spoke of my soul's purpose and what I could do to honor God in my work. He reminded me that sometimes to achieve the highest goal, one must walk alone against the majority in their beliefs, with faith being their only companion.

He was not presumptious, but humble, and spoke with such compassion and conviction, that I felt the truth of His heart penetrate mine.

His name was Jesus of Nazareth. And when He left me that day, he gave me His blessing, which never left me. So I became one of the Magi, honoring Him, spreading his love whenever and wherever I could.

The lion and the lamb had met, and yet to me, He was not a God, but a man who truly loved all with no limit, with the greatest heart I had ever known.

I knew I was not anyone special. I was just an ordinary young woman with an old soul. Many times I would argue with Matheu, that I was unworthy of this attention. But he said that in my innocence and openness, it had come to me, and through my dedication it had grown. I worked at it, always setting aside the majority of my day to work with spirit, including them in every aspect of my life. After all, they had raised me.

I did not calculate what was happening to me in terms of power. To me spirit was family. The guides taught me that true power cannot be measured in worldly things, such as money or possessions.

True power is limitless love, which becomes a source of inspiration and hope to all who seek it. It does not want for itself, but receives and returns what it gets, in conjunction with the ebb and flow of the universe. True power multiplies by letting go, it does not hoard. True power always acknowledges its source, which is the Source Of All Things. It spreads like a network through everyone in body or out, through the dimensions, bonding all to each other and to this greater being, from which all things come. True power is family that extends beyond blood into the soul, which knows no boundaries. Each and every person has a special birthright, and is a part of that greater family.

Every time I sat down to channel, I was surrounded by an intense white light, which filled me with that power, and infused me with that love, feeding my soul, as I acknowledged my birthright and who I truly was, and gave thanks to God for it. I could feel the source flowing through my veins, and I truly became my Father's daughter.

Spirit taught me that in order to create my own reality, I must first become a part of that flow, instead of trying to control it. So God became a living parent, instead of a myth, and I became a part of Him, and the greater river of His love .

My reality was very different from the majority of the world's. To me, spirit was not intangible, but visible, and I could talk as easily to a guide as I could talk to anyone. Most of my friends were channels, for they shared my vision. Yet I never tried to convince an unbeliever, knowing that they must grow in their own time.

When I was little, the world seemed very big, and I had never ventured beyond the boundaries of my home and Pennsylvania, for I was afraid to get lost. Now the universe seemed very small, as I was united to everyone and everything in it. Though I was but a very small stream leading to that greater ocean, the tide always took me there, and returned me home safely, with loving arms.

The universe became my home, and I began to physically travel more in conjunction with my work, either to study or to teach, but mostly to share, for everyone knows one always learns from teaching and is always a student.

I had everything and more, yet there was a part of me that hungered for physical arms to share my life with, for I had left my marriage behind a long time ago.

This feeling began to intensify as the green warmth of summer changed to the cooler colors of fall. I began to dream of a man on a horse, who would come for me, as a knight in shining armor would come for his lady fair. Matheu simply said teasingly that one day soon my prince would come, and he would have some competition.

Late September, when the leaves were beginning to turn into nature's rainbow, I left Pennsylvania on a journey to a distant state called Arizona. Arizona was a far away place in the West, completely opposite from my natural surroundings in the East. Where Pennsylvania grew lush rolling hills of green that softened the horizon and the soul, Arizona grew great mountains of stone, and dry deserts with thorny plants, that tested nature and one's spirit, rather than refreshing it.

I was invited there to attend a seminar on healing. So I left my children at the home of their father, and with Matheu, headed out West.

When I arrived, I found myself in a city, much like all the other cities I had been to. But country girl that I was, I was filled with a longing to be out in the wide open spaces.

After the seminar, at Matheu's suggestion, I left the buildings and parking lots behind me, and began to drive to the desert and the mountains. Instinctively, I headed towards the Superstition Mountains. They loomed before me as I approached them, brazenly breaking up the horizon. They were huge and forboding; brown against the blue of the sky.

There was a riding stable there that provided horses to explore the mountains and cowboys to take you out safely and back. So I went riding in the land of the Superstition Mountains, testing ground of the soul, like the Indians before me.

I was up very high in the mountains, and felt as if I were flying on the rocky slopes which held my horse and myself. The narrow path was lined with cactus, and the horizon was nothing but desert. One cowboy began to talk to me, and as I responded, I heard Matheu say, "You are talking to the wrong cowboy." I turned my head and saw him.

He appeared to be slightly younger, and in his quiet solitude, he seemed a part of the mountains which stood behind him.

There was a boldness about him as he surveyed the horizon, and he was more like an eagle, perched on a mountain top ready to fly, silent, but aware, and speaking with his every move.

He rode his horse with a graceful fluidity that made him seem suspended in mid air. Man, animal and mountain were one in that moment. He had reddish brown hair, and dark eyes that sparkled with their depth, and were wishing wells to his soul and greater mysteries. And with all his stern strength, there was a strange innocence about him. He was protector, and vulnerable, at the same time. I felt a strange sense of belonging as he looked at me, that carried me beyond myself. I was safe with him, as I had been with Matheu before him.

We spoke of many things that day, quietly and serenely. With no effort or struggle, our oneness was attained almost instantly. We rode together forever, as the day turned into dusk, and the mountains paled pink against the setting sun, and even the desert softened in that light.

When I was thirsty, he gave me drink, for he knew where to find water in the desert, which to the eye held none. When I was tired, we climbed from our horses, and he spread a blanket for me to rest upon. And when my soul cried out for softness, in the barren mountains which held no roses, he found one. He dismounted and cut me a mountain flower, a prickly pear cactus bud, which when cut bears not only beauty, but fruit. He sustained me in that desert, not only with the knowledge of his surroundings, but by his presence. I didn't know it then, but in those first few hours, he became a part of me and I of him.

The two halves of our soul had come together from dimensions unknown on that mountain top, in the physical form of two children, one having known great love in life, one not having known love at all, but meeting it for the first time. Together we formed one being, in darkness and in light, so very different from each other, yet almost the same. Like Siamese twins, we became inseperable from that moment on, both physically and spiritually, under the eyes of Heaven, in the arms of the mountain and in our own hearts.

Song of The Cowboy

I was born in England out of emotional wedlock. They were legally married, but not committed to each other or to me. My father was a drunk and violent man. He was a fighter pilot in the American Armed Forces stationed overseas. He was a Top Gun at home and at work. My mother was a frail person, who couldn't quite get it all together to take care of us, let alone herself. She couldn't understand my father's drunken fits. She kept trying to win his approval, but never got it.

I was too young to really understand what was going on between them, but I knew more than they gave me credit for. I felt what was going on, and a lot of times I was afraid of what would happen.

He had other women on the side and he would go to bars, leaving us out in the cold. A lot of times he would come home drunk, and there would be an argument, then he would hurt her. They say he was a better soldier than husband and father. "Women are nothing but a piece of meat," he would say. My little baby brother was too young to understand the words, but I did.

This is where I got my start in life. My mother tried to nurture us, but was too upset most of the time. She took pills for her nerves, maybe she got addicted to them, I don't know. The only safe feeling I felt was on my mother's lap when she would hold me. It calmed us both down. She bought me my first horse, and I would climb on his back and ride away into the sunset, like the American cowboys I used to watch on television. I was happy on my horse and on my mother's lap.

My mother's nerves got worse. Friends looked after us a lot of the time, but it didn't stay that way for very long, and one day I remember being brought to the Children's Home with my baby brother. I didn't have my horse with me to ride away into the sunset.

I can still smell my mother's perfume, hear the swooshing of her skirt against her stockings, and feel her arms through her sweater hugging me. She said she would be back for us. I remember watching that big, black car pull away with her inside it and trying to chase it, screaming for it to stop. My brother was too young to remember.

My mother never came back for us, and neither did my father. They must have forgotten. From that moment on I was alone. And I was very angry at them, the world and God.

I was born dead. There was no other way out for me. All I knew was anger and fear. The people at the home say I was hungry for love and attention, because I would do things and get into a lot of trouble, but they were wrong.

I felt like a freak or a test tube baby, born without a soul, because after that I couldn't feel anything. No matter who would offer me friendship or affection, I pulled away, so I grew up empty and feeling disconnected from everything.

I was small for my size, but strong. I always got into fights, to prove myself. I learned early in life to look after myself. I tried looking after my brother, but he was different than me. He seemed to fit in with other people. He was happier. I didn't want to fit in, because I didn't want to be a part of anything. I didn't allow anyone in, not since she left me.

Each hand me down, or worn toy, became a prized possession that I would keep all to myself. No one touched me or my things. At night, I would dream of big, black cars taking someone away, and I would wake, screaming and sweating with nothing to hold onto. Sometimes, I would dream of being a cowboy, riding my horse again, away from everything.

Mostly I acted cold and distant, but I could act sweet too, to get what I wanted, and they wouldn't know I was pretending. They didn't know that I didn't feel anything, and didn't really care about anyone.

There were people along the way who tried to get into my heart. Counselors, teachers and other kids in my group who had also been abandoned. Sometimes I pretended to care about them, sometimes I didn't, depending on the mood I was in, but the feeling never returned. I was numb. They taught us, they fed us, they clothed us, and they sent us to church, but they didn't really love us, nobody did, not God, not man, or why would they have left us here?

22

The years passed and I grew up into a young man with no identity. By that I mean I was myself, but not connected to anything else. I was from nowhere and going nowhere. I had no home in this world.

I had some talent as an artist. With my pen I could draw sketches that were pretty good. I liked music too, especially individual singers, like Elvis and Johnny Mathis. They seemed to feel what they were singing. I didn't like to read, and wasn't good at schoolwork. It seemed like a waste of time to me. I had no future or anything, so what was the point of studying?

I didn't have a whole lot of opportunity to pursue a career in art or music, because there was no training or tools provided. There were no extras there, just the bare basics of a practical life.

Throwaway people can't find themselves, because somebody has already decided, be it God or their parents, that they aren't worth anything. I didn't really care anyway, because most of what I drew or sang was an imitation of something or somebody. I copied real life in my art, I didn't create it. Everything came from without, nothing came from within, because there was no feeling there.

A bigger boy tried to touch me once. He climbed into my bed, but I pushed him away and got into a fight, and the counselors punished me for causing trouble. I can't stand being touched by anyone, even girls. Women are nothing but trouble.

As I grew older, a local man took an interest in me and my brother. He was unmarried and looked after his elderly parents. He was a teacher and active in community affairs. Somebody had told him of the two boys who had been there for so long without any family to care about them. The other kids sometimes got adopted or placed with other relatives. They had connections in the world and we didn't.

This man started to visit us, and we got to know one another. Pretty soon he was taking us home on overnight passes to his family home. It was a quiet house on a quiet street, in an average neighborhood, mostly families with children, and elderly people in a world of their own. It had all those fine touches that you would think of to make a proper home, like soft pillows and knick knacks scattered about.

It was a home to dream about, and even though at first I felt uncomfortable in it, I soon began to like it and wanted more and more of it. I mean there was something warm about it compared to the starkness of the Children's Home. It smelled of cooking, and though it wasn't grand or anything, it had all the comforts that the children's home didn't have. We had our own room, and my brother and I began to spend more time there.

I suppose we were very lucky and I should have been grateful. He and his parents were good people. They were the family I never had. But I felt apart from everything, and even though I knew they cared about us, I still didn't feel anything inside. But I liked the image of having a family, and I began to feel like an actor in a play or a movie, playing the role of being a part of something.

This is where I learned things most people take for granted. Like eating in a restaurant, having clean clothes that matched, or going to the movies and the theatre. We had chores, and would help with the dinner and the cleaning up afterwards. My brother and I finally had a connection in the real world other than ourselves.

I had trouble with it though, mostly because it didn't seem real to me. This was a family who was offering me something to believe in, but I wasn't buying any of it. I still remembered my mother leaving me, and knew that was the reality. I mean if someone gives you real roses, then takes them away, and later on replaces them with those artificial plastic flowers, saying they might last longer, you would feel the same.

So even though we eventually began to live there, I didn't believe in it. On the outside it may have looked real, but it wasn't the same. I always kept my distance on the inside, even though they never knew. I couldn't count on anything or anyone.

I knew this could end just like before. This man tried to give me everything that I never had, but he was not my real father, and wanting it to be different didn't change a thing. But, I did what I usually did. I pretended to feel something, when truly I didn't feel anything. I was just trying to get by and get some more of the things that I wanted.

I guess you could say in many ways I was a typical teenager. I worshipped Elvis, and wore my hair in a slicked back version of that style. I got into trouble sometimes, because it seemed that no matter how much I had, I wanted more. Nothing was enough to fill that big, black hole within me, for I always felt empty inside. So, I tried to fill myself with things from the outside. Once in a great while, I would steal small things from the house, and sell them for money to buy what I wanted. I knew if I got caught, I would be punished. But it didn't really matter, because I didn't really care.

You see, what no one understood was that I was not a part of anything or anyone, and no matter what they did, it couldn't hurt me, because they were strangers. Everbody was a stranger to me and that is the way I wanted it to be.

Nothing could hurt me anymore because I didn't love them or anyone, God included. I was all alone in the world and I wanted to keep it that way. When I was being punished, I learned the rules, but I didn't believe in them. And when I was being praised, I didn't believe in that either.

My philosophy was like a convict's code. It was merely a matter of survival. Nothing was real, nothing lasted, and there was nothing to believe in.

I started to sneak a drink back then, all the kids did. But for me it was different because when I drank, I felt better, like I could be someone else. When I was drunk, my heart felt lighter. Even though I wasn't able to drink all the time, when I did, I felt like I had found faith or God. The only religion I ever knew was in those good feelings, and it felt good to finally feel something, even though it came from a bottle.

There was a part of me that I never talked about. It was the part of me that loved that rocking horse and would ride it forever. This man must have known, because he gave me a small statue of a horse, which I always kept with me, I don't know why. I guess it showed me that he cared. But mostly I knew that it represented my future, because I was sure I would be a cowboy someday.

I identified with that strong stern figure that had no home, just what he carried on his horse. The cowboy never stayed in one place for very long, and lived free from any ties. He didn't need anyone or anything, and was completely self sufficient. Even though he stayed alone, everyone respected and feared him. The world was his home, and he slept outside under the stars, killed his own food, and cooked his grub himself. He didn't need a woman and if he did, there was always a saloon not too far off, with a warm bed, a pretty girl, and a jug of whiskey to meet his needs for a small price. His life was more than enough, for he only believed in himself, nothing else.

I dreamed more and more of this as time went on, while I was doing other things, and pretty soon I could think of nothing else. John Wayne was my Jesus, and I lived for his movies. I made up my mind to go to America, and make my way West, where no one or nothing could touch me again.

See, cowboys have no feelings, they don't need them. They have no roots and they don't want to build anything or become anyone. They have no past or future because they just exist within themselves in the moment. They don't need a mother or God, and nothing can hurt them. Anything that gets in their way regrets it. I wanted to lose myself in that image, so no one could find me. The image again became more important than the reality I was in.

It was about that time the Children's Home contacted me. My mother wanted to see us. I didn't want to see her, but did it for the sake of my brother. I was really nervous, I don't know why. She came one rainy day with her boyfriend. When she walked into the room, I didn't feel a thing. Just some twinges in my stomach. She was very pretty. I wanted to be angry, and tell her off, but I couldn't do it. I stared at her and tried to memorize her face down to the last detail. She cried and promised me that she would come back soon and we would get closer. She said she left us because she was sick, but would make it up to us. But I didn't believe her. My brother did.

As it turned out, she never came back again. Weeks, then months passed, and we never heard a word from her. Maybe she was still sick. It's a good thing I didn't care, or I would have really been hurt. To walk out on your kids twice in one lifetime is too much in my opinion. Anyway, maybe my father was right when he told me women are nothing.

All I knew was I had to get out of there. When the Children's Home found my father living in California and he invited us to come, I said yes. It was my way out West, and besides, I was curious. I mean it was my mother's fault that I was the way I was. It was time to meet the old man and get on with my life.

My adopted father was upset. I guess he was hoping that I wouldn't go, but the truth was I had to. I cared for him in my own way, more than anyone I had ever known in my life. I was grateful to him for what he had done for me, but, I had to find out the truth about myself, and I couldn't trust anyone anymore.

The only reason I was anywhere was because I had been born. I didn't have any choice in my life. Everybody had made my choices for me. First my parents, then the Children's Home, and then my adopted father. Nobody asked me what I wanted or needed, and I wanted out. I'm glad they said they cared, but I didn't really believe in them. I didn't believe in God either, because if there really was a God and he cared, then why would he let my mother throw me away?

I was out of there, heading West to the home of the free and the brave, and I wasn't looking back. We took a plane to California, and my father picked us up. I looked like him. He took us to a nice suburban home and gave us our own rooms. He wasn't rich or anything, but he earned a good living, so we were able to buy things we never had before. He was a strange man in many ways. He seemed glad to see us, but the only time he would ever really talk to us was when he had been drinking. During the week he would go to work, come home, and watch television. He would be stone cold silent. But on the weekends he would get very drunk and talk his head off, then pass out, or, go to some bar and get into an argument, and we would have to go and bring him home. Then Monday would come, and he would start work again. It was the same thing over and over.

He couldn't seem to be nice to both of us at the same time. He would play favorites, between me and my brother, and it made me wonder why. Maybe there was only so much love to go around in this world. I sure wasn't getting my share of it.

He blamed my mother for leaving us. He said it wasn't his fault. My brother and he actually got along. I didn't believe him at all.

I hated the way he was, and the fact that every time I looked at him, he reminded me of myself. I knew he couldn't feel anything either. It was all a con job, or he wouldn't have left us in the first place. I didn't want to see that, so I started planning my escape. I had some money saved up and decided I was going to leave and make my own way in the world. I wanted to be a cowboy, so I decided to go to Wyoming. He didn't try to stop me either. So I packed up my gear, and left for Wyoming to start my new life. And for the first time, I felt hope.

I didn't have much trouble hitching rides there. It was almost as if the fates were helping me. Once I got there, that was when the trouble started. I had no place to stay, and wound up sleeping in a field outside of town. I tried getting a job as a hand on a couple of ranches, but couldn't get hired because I had no experience. I started to drink a lot back then, just to pass the time. Wyoming has a ton of cowboy bars, and in my new clothes and hat, I felt like I had been born again. Finally, when I was just about to run out of money and luck, I got hired on at a small horse ranch on the outskirts of town. This is where I really learned my trade. I was a natural in the saddle, and got along better with animals than with people. But I made those animals do what I wanted, because no dumb animal was going to control me. I cleaned up horse shit out of horse pens, learned how to rope and ride, and did my share of blacksmithing. There was an old man who had worked there for years and he taught me. I sort of pretended that he was my grandfather in my mind. It made me feel like I belonged there.

Most of the time it was backbreaking work of fixing fence, hauling hay and water to feed, and then cleaning up and hauling manure, over and over again. But the best part was when I was riding, free with the wind blowing in my face, my hat almost falling off my head, with nothing to hold me back, or, get in my way. I felt like I was flying to Heaven or somewhere, and was a part of something greater than I was. For the first time, I felt happy, but then the horse would stop, and I would have to come back to earth, fixing fence, hauling hay and manure, and it would hurt again. The only thing I could do would be to have a drink or two in town, until the whole thing started over the next day.

Wages were cheap and hours long, but I didn't care. I had a bed in a bunkhouse and free grub, and the old man had given me a broken down saddle of my own. He taught me how to fix it, so I started practicing doing leather work. At first it was hard. I only made small things, but it felt good being able to create something I could see with my own hands. Some of the emptiness I always felt inside began to fade, with those little doodads I made, and riding on my horse.

I wasn't really interested in women. I picked a couple up once in a while, just to get laid, but they were more trouble than they were worth. All they did was use you for sex, and to buy them drinks, then move on to the next guy. I was happier by myself.

I got a German Shepherd pup, and I raised her by hand. I was everything to her, the mother she never knew, and she was my family. God pity anyone coming near me because she would eat them alive. That's the way I trained my Sheba.

One night I was very tired, and was sitting in the bunkhouse drinking by myself, with a bottle of whiskey and some beers, when a neighbor boy came in to borrow a radio from one of the family in the main house. Nobody was home, and I knew the guy, so I went in and got it, and gave it to him.

I didn't think anything of it, but drank until I passed out. The next morning the sheriff came and arrested me for stealing. I told them about the neighbor boy, but he lied and denied getting the radio. He said he didn't even come over and his family covered for him. They said I made it up just to save myself. After all, he was somebody and I was nobody. I came from nothing and was going nowhere.

I tried to fight it, but I had no real friends. My adopted father in England tried to help and so did my natural father in California, but nobody believed them. I was a drifter. The cards were stacked against me, stealing was a felony, and Wyoming had a hanging judge at that time. "Two years," he said. Before I could even spit, I wound up in the federal penitentiary, serving time for a crime I didn't commit. I had to leave my dog where I got her for awhile. I hoped she wouldn't forget me like everyone else had. This is what I mean about having no choice. God had thrown me away again for no reason. After that, I didn't care if I lived or died.

There was a girl I had met at one of the bars, who came from a local family. She had taken a shine to me, and was always trying to get me to take her out. She reminded me of my mother. Her family was religious, but she could be a wildcat at those bars, flirting with the guys, though her family never knew.

She always went to church on Sunday. Well, she heard about what happened, and came to see me every visiting day. She was very kind, but in my opinion, sort of spoiled and bossy. Without her back then, I would have been lost. She brought me homemade cookies to make up for the prison grub, and made me laugh. She gave me something to look forward to.

By then, because of good behavior, they had moved me to a minimum security prison, a work farm, to serve out the rest of my sentence. I was glad to get out of that rat hole of a state pen, where people try to poke you in the ass for fun, and steal your food. Not quite like the Children's Home I grew up in, but somewhat similar, because in both places you have no identity, and nobody really cares if you live or die.

Anyway, I wasn't really courting her, because that wasn't my way. But she was courting me. She made up her mind to have me, and I was in no position to argue. Besides, I kind of liked her. She was wild and free, yet nice at the same time. We got along. I usually went along with things when I had no other choice and when they were in my best interest, so I went along with this. When she asked about love, I didn't know what to say. I hated that word. She made me feel good, but I would never use that word for anyone. It didn't mean a thing to me. I was happy around her, and she had what I wanted, which was security.

She came from a good family that had their own place outside of town, and I could be a part of something more than myself. I might be somebody, so this could never happen to me again. So, if that was love, then I was in love.

I don't believe in no fairy tales, and I figured this was the best I could do for myself. So when I got parole after eighteen months, we decided to get married. We got married before I could even get the bars out of my mind.

I got my dog back right away, and she didn't forget me. Sheba was still the best family I ever had, more loyal than a woman could ever be.

My wife's family accepted me because they had to. She always got her own way. She reminded me of myself, because she knew how to play the game. Before I even knew it, she was pregnant. Now that really shocked me, because I didn't want a family. It reminded me of what my mother had done to me, and I didn't want that to happen to any other kid.

I started to feel edgy and cooped up, so I began to take a lot of wrangling jobs away from her, living somewhere else, and coming home occasionally on my days off. Have saddle, will travel. No woman was ever going to own me. While I was at work at these jobs, I began to wonder what she was doing behind my back, maybe just like my mother did to my father.

When I would go home, I started to hate it, and drink more and more, becoming angrier and angrier, until I started to rough her up a little bit, calling her names, and pushing her around.

It was a daughter, and when she was born, I felt proud of my part in it. She was like a little puppy dog to me, and I took care of her the best I could. But I wasn't into this nurturing stuff, because I didn't know how. No one had ever nurtured me.

Sometimes I would take off for days at a time, drinking and carousing, and then come home to a major fight. I wasn't sure if I belonged there anymore. A part of me wanted out, but instead of leaving I drank more and more, and got meaner. But, it wasn't long before that marriage was over. She threw me out, and I was glad to go. I guess I drove her to it. I gave her an uncontested divorce with no custody for me. It was better that way, as if it had never happened.

It was over and my father had been right, women are nothing but a piece of meat. My daughter was better off with her mother, because no child should be separated from their mother. Any mother is better than no mother at all. Believe me, I know.

I made up my mind then and there to leave Wyoming and go to Arizona. I didn't want any part of them. It shouldn't have happened in the first place, and I didn't look back. I heard that she remarried and was going to have another child. I suppose another man suited them better, so I guess it wasn't love after all, for as I hear it, love lasts. I wasn't hurt or sad. I was angry, because I was tired of being the bad one in this world.

So I packed my gear, including the old saddle, and me and my dog headed in my old pickup truck to Arizona, to make a fresh start, glad to be rid of them all.

It seemed to take forever getting there, driving down winding highways, with this pain in my gut that was eating me alive. Nothing seemed real to me, for everywhere I went, things went wrong. I couldn't seem to find a place of my own to call home. That was when I decided to change my name.

I wanted to be a different person that had nothing to do with my past. I called myself John, because it was strong and simple, and like everybody else. Nobody would ever know who *I* was, or where I came from. The old me was dead, and I would never go back to those people who had pretended to care. I gave myself a nickname, which was JJ, and I was reborn.

As I kept driving, the countryside began to change from green to desert. With the change in scenery, and my new name, I began to feel better about what had happened. I knew I didn't belong in Wyoming, but in Arizona, and I began to look forward to what was to come.

When I got to Phoenix, I started looking around for a place to work and live. I had slept in my truck for a couple of nights, stretched out in the truck bed with my head in the stars, a million miles away from those that had hurt me. By then I was almost broke. I was very tired and I hadn't had a drink for awhile, and boy was it hot. But there was something about the desert that made me feel at home. It calmed my nature, for even though it was rough country, it was beautiful in its own way. I liked rough country. The meaner it was, the better it was for me.

At a bar, some guy told me about a riding stable in the Superstition Mountains that hired on wranglers to take people out in the mountains for hourly rides or overnights, so I thought I would try to find a job there.

The people at the stable were real friendly. They were very short of help, it being the busy season, when the winter tourists and the wannabe cowboys come to whoop it up. I gave them my new name, and made up a story about having an old grandfather in Wyoming, who had a small ranch. I told them I was trying to make my way in the world to help him save his ranch. I had a good gift of gab, and didn't want anyone to know the truth, that I was nothing and had nothing. They believed me, and I got hired on right away.

They gave me a tiny, mice infested, dirty room, with an old mattress over the horse stalls in the barn, but I didn't care about that because I finally had a place of my own.

I loved the mountains, because you always felt danger everywhere, from riding on the sides of deep canyons, on rocky slopes that could take a horse down with one misstep, to the thorny growth that covered every trail. One wrong move and you and your horse would have cactus up your ass. I loved the feeling of isolation, for you could ride forever, hot and dusty, cutting out a trail and never really getting there. The land and the freedom never stopped and the wild went on forever. Sometimes I felt like the only living creature in the world. I wasn't afraid of the danger, but courted it, and dared it to touch me. I was tougher than it was, and loved shooting rattlesnakes that threatened me with my gun. My dog instinctively knew every trail, and she led the way. Sheba and I were a team.

I loved guiding the people because they looked up to me. To them I was some sort of hero, the strong wrangler, protecting them from nature and guiding them home to safety. I was in control of them. They had to do what I said, or they wouldn't make it home. Most of them were terrified of horses, and sat with their big butts clinging to the saddle horn, afraid for their lives.

I laughed at them. They had no clue as to what was really going on out there or in my mind. With my gift of gab, I could bullshit them into believing anything. I would be complimenting a woman on her riding, encouraging her to move her horse forward, and thinking at the same time, what a fat ugly bitch she was, sitting on that poor horse like a sack of shit.

Everyday was like that, enjoying where I was, pretending I was a hero, conning the guests, and at night I would fix up my room, cleaning up the mice shit, and trying to make it feel more like home.

One early September morning, I walked out on the front porch of the stable and saw her sitting there. She was waiting to be taken out on a day's ride with another wrangler. I don't know why, but I couldn't take my eyes off her. I kept looking at her out of the corner of my eye, sizing her up, as I tried to act casual, smoking my cigarette and staring out at the mountains, coolly adjusting the spurs on my boots.

She was beautiful, but not in the way I usually thought. She was different looking. Most of the women I went out with were hard looking, and kind of looked the same. It's hard to describe, but she seemed soft, and comfortable in her face and body.

It was almost as if an old fashioned painting had come to life. For a minute, she didn't seem real, only a mirage of times past. But she didn't disappear. She had long, dark hair, and dark dreamy eyes, that somehow, when you looked in them, you felt like you could drown. She had a wide forties smile that lit up her whole face. You could forget yourself simply by staring at her.

She was funny too, because she had her long hair gathered up into one ponytail that stuck out on the side of her head, like a deer with an antler cut off. She was very quiet and shy, but seemed composed within herself, as she smiled at me while I stood there.

It was a real moment, the first I'd ever had, and I wanted it to last forever. Something stuck in my gut right then. *I* didn't know what it was, but it seemed like I knew her, or wanted to know *her*. For some reason, I didn't want to let her out of my sight, so I casually offered to my boss to take the ride out myself.

I had never felt love, didn't want to feel love, and had no intention of ever feeling love. I wasn't going to change my mind about that. I didn't care about something I had never had, and

34

probably would never have. My parents had taught me that, and I had learned that lesson very well. Everything I touched turned to dirt instead of gold in my whole life, and like I said before, I didn't believe in no fairy tales. I didn't believe in anyone or anything.

But, there was something about her, whether it was the shyness, or the compassion in her voice when she spoke that felt like a cool breeze in the summer heat, or maybe, it was her eyes that were deeper than the Thames. It might have been that wide smile, or that antler sticking out of the side of her head, but I wanted to touch her and be touched by her at the same time.

So I got on my horse, and took the lead in the ride, with her following right behind me on a gentle mare to match her personality. A couple of dudes followed behind her, with another wrangler riding shotgun behind them.

She obviously had ridden before, because she rode lightly and moved with the horse. She didn't hold onto the saddle horn at all, but boy was she scared of heights. The other wrangler scolded her a couple of times as we got to higher ground, with great drops beside us into open canyons, because she tried to close her eyes. I didn't say a word to her. I wanted her to notice me like I had noticed her. I felt like telling her I would catch her if she fell, but I held back, so I wouldn't make a fool of myself. She seemed out of my league.

The other cowboy was flirting up a storm with her, talking a mile a minute, when all of a sudden, out of the blue, she turned to me and asked me my name. We started to talk, and for the rest of that day I showed her my world, and she told me about hers.

I guess you could say we both came from two different worlds. She came from back east and from culture, and I was all wild west. She had a family and I had none. She was into this space cadet stuff, and all I cared about was what was happening right now, under my feet.

But somehow, it seemed like we were the same, and came from the same place. When we were together, there was no world. Nothing mattered except us, our world, with just the two of us in it. It was as if we belonged to each other, and even

35

though I didn't believe in love, or God, I believed in her from that moment on.

Song of The Earth

To them, time and distance didn't matter. Nothing seemed to get in the way of their relationship and the bond that held them together.

He could not leave his mountain, not having the means, but she was like quicksilver and with spirit helping her, she found whatever was necessary to fly to see him. More and more frequently she went, staying for longer periods as time went on, unwilling to leave, yet unable to stay, because of other obligations.

He was always watching and waiting for her visits, at first hoping more business would bring her there, and then, just encouraging her to come for no reason at all. The time in between was filled with a mix of emptiness and the yearning to fill that emptiness with the elation of being together again, until finally, he just expected her there, as if that were her home, and anywhere else did not exist.

She carried both worlds within her wherever she was, her children in the East and he in the West, together in her heart as if there was no space between them. Like a weathervane pivoting on a barn roof, she changed direction, but was always constant in her love for them all.

He was volatile and vibrant, while she was soft and gentle. They were very different in nature, yet they were linked together by an indescribable bond that was stronger than steel and could not be broken.

There were those that did not understand what drew them to each other, and there were those that did. Either way, neither cared, for they could not seem to survive alone.

They both struggled in their own way with their feelings, trying to understand why they were so important to each other. Neither of them had ever experienced anything like it before in any previous relationship. It was indefinable, yet defined everything they did or felt. Everything else seemed small and unimportant compared to it.

She likened it to the unconditional love of her children or of the guides, and the feeling she felt when channeling. He likened it to a very small memory he had of his mother before she abandoned him, before the pain and the anger had devoured his soul. To her it was a torch, to him it was a glimmer of hope.

It was both a joy and a hardship at the same time. It was the easiest thing either of them had ever done, yet, it was also the hardest, for the modern world does not acknowledge nor honor the true heart, but prefers to bless the surface, based on appearances and backgrounds.

If the modern world had its way, she would have met a conservative man, while he would have found a cowgirl.

But they lived in a dimension far greater than the average person, for she was a channel of the light, and he was a part of her. Neither one could find any peace in that shallow judgement, and both without hesitation found themselves in deeper dimensions, choosing the highest path of unconditional love, led by their souls on the path of the heart.

As the guides explained to her, the highest path is the path of the heart. They spoke not of the human heart, for that is fickle and changes constantly based upon the needs of the personality.

"I love him because he is filling my needs at this time. I don't love him when he is not doing that, but I have met another who is like he was at the beginning of our relationship, and he is meeting my needs, so, maybe I love him instead. But is this really love?" pleads the human heart.

The cycle of questioning, "Is this really love?" continues without the question ever being answered. Each person is focused upon the heart of the personality, whose false rhythm charges the physical world with constantly changing perceptions of love.

Those that solely follow the physical path never know the true heart, the heart of their soul, which never changes or skips a beat, and whose constant rhythm reinforces our path and our progress, emulating the unconditional love of God, his guides and the Christ within.

Those that hear that heartbeat in harmony with another's soul, are dancing to the rhythm of true love and to those dancers of the heart, great love is possible that lasts beyond the boundaries of this lifetime into eternity, despite the illusions of the physical world.

To find one's true heart, one must let go of the human heart and all the expectations that it bears. One must get beyond third dimensional reality and linear time, whose boundaries bind you, into the higher dimensions of timelessness, which will free you and is where the true heart of the soul resides.

To become the multidimensional people that we are meant to be, we must remember the truth of our own identity. Our lifetimes in body are very short, compared to the eternal life of our souls. We are not really physical people who have a soul, but instead, we are souls temporarily residing as physical people. We must begin to see ourselves and others as who we truly are, and not just what we appear to be. Instead of living the illusion, we must live the truth. It is then and only then, that our question of "Is it love," can be answered and that eternal love, instead of temporal love, can come to us without end.

To walk the highest path, one must put aside all preconceived notions and boundaries placed there by the limitations of the personality and by society, which is composed of many similar limited personalities. You must look beyond the physical illusion into the truth of the soul to live your love.

At times, there will be judgement from those who do not see what you see, and who choose to stay limited in their vision and their way of thinking. The illusion may be more comfortable for them than the truth.

Life becomes a paradox, where what you see is not always what you will believe in, where for others, what they see firmly establishes their belief system. For them, someone who looks good is better than someone who is good.

Many choose to remain boxed in the world with the lid firmly on. Their world becomes that box. They limit themselves and their vision. But God's gift to man is free will and they have that right to deny themselves their own vision and their own heritage. Like a bird never leaving its nest to fly free, they remain grounded by their fears and expectations, and the illusion that what they are experiencing is all that there is. They will only

39

experience conditional love, for they cannot see beyond the walls they have built for themselves.

For those who seek a deeper love, they must leave behind all prejudices and limitations, which are untrue and come only from ignorance, fear and pain, and move from that small world of limited love into that broader universe of unconditional love, which knows no end. The bird must fly free to reach the greatest height.

The world is filled with broken marrages, for most unions are based upon the temporal needs of the personality and the shifting emotions of the human heart. It is from a deeper space that marriage vows can take on a new meaning. For those on the path of the heart, marriage becomes a perpetual and neverending union, for it is not based upon the physical and temporary existence, but on the love of the souls, which extend before and after this one lifetime of experience. Physical limitations will have no effect for it is no longer till death do us part, for there is no death to a soul union. Just as God's love knows no end, so is His legacy to them.

This is not for everyone. One must be ready for this path, in body, mind and spirit. One must find that special partner, who is also at the correct stage of their own growth. It must be mutually desired and achieved.

Most marriages are made on earth for the short term satisfaction of the people involved, instead of on the soul level. Some souls may choose to remain alone, complete in themselves, while only entering into temporary unions to facilitate their own lessons of growth and that of others. They will create family structures that span the eons of time, but never merge with just one other soul.

Every one in time is different and situations of a true soul partnership are far and few between. But occasionally, a special union is born, one that has no beginning and knows no end, because the two souls are made for each other, despite what the various physical incarnations might bring.

Sometimes, to follow the path of the heart, you must walk alone in the midst of strangers who are incapable of understanding, judging by their own shallow, limited experiences. At times there is danger, for the physical reality is constantly changing, as people give way to the needs of their personalities. They may lash out at those who they perceive to be different. One must be willing to sacrifice their physical comfort for a soul love on the path of the heart. But, as others have done before you, you may find strength from within and from God to survive. You must have faith in your love. Christ walked the path of the heart for all mankind.

Ultimately, you must trust in the path, knowing that your reward may lie on the other side of this mortal existence, for all sides are the same to the soul. Both partners must believe in each other, no matter what comes and be willing to risk all for that belief. That is the path of the heart.

As she struggled to understand what was happening, Matheu explained it to her in simplified terms.

He told her they were not soulmates, which was nothing more than an overused term with a misunderstood meaning in the physical world.

Each and every soul had developed relationships over time and through reincarnation with other souls. Thus, the term soulmates meant nothing more than forming a bond with a near or distant relative, that one has known throughout other lifetimes and that one has felt close to. These bonds are very common, and happen every day, for every soul has connections from the past.

Some soulmate bonds are closer than others, just as some family members are closer to each other in the physical reality. Some are more distant. Each are unique in their relationships.

Just as we are born into physical families, souls have families also, that are constantly reincarnating together throughout time, supporting and propelling each other by previous agreement through their earthly lessons to become, ultimately, better souls.

But what they were experiencing was very different from that, for not all souls are part of a soul family, having progressed beyond that level in their growth to stand on their own. What they were experiencing seldom occured. Theirs was an inseperable bond, that was extremely rare universally, and that never changed, for it was the bond of soul twins. She settled back in her chair as the great guide prepared to tell her the story of their souls.

"Close your eyes and listen carefully to me, for I will tell you the story of your true legacy, and though you may not fully understand it, you will begin to see the depth of your lineage throughout time and the dimensions of reality, and how it all has come together to affect you today," Matheu said.

"Imagine a soul as a huge tree, whose arms are many strong branches reaching up to the sky, with many leaves filling those branches. That tree is your soul, the soul of Astarte, from whom you get your name, and the source of your strength. She is one of the old ones, for she comes from the beginning of time, and gets her strength directly from the source, which you know as God. Those souls that come from the beginning, stand with the angelic realm and were appointed guardians and teachers of the younger souls."

"She always stood alone, displaying exemplary character in her service to God and to mankind. She was complete within herself, content to accomplish her own lessons, and resolute in her service to God as he desired. There came a time when she desired companionship, and because of her devotion to God and the stature of her service, she was granted permission to have a mate."

"Contained within God is everything in perfect balance. The masculine and the feminine, the positive and the negative, the darkness and the light are all within Him. Even evil comes from God, to accent the good, and to allow his children a choice in their growth through the gift of free will. All souls are born of God in his own image. They are also complete within themselves. Some choose to walk alone, content with accomplishing and achieving their own lessons in an independent manner, while only developing temporary connections and relationships as needed within their soul families. These relationships are designed to assist in their continuing spiritual growth. But, once in a great while, a soul union is born, with the permission of the Creator for the highest good, for those souls whose extraordinary qualities have earned it and who desire it more than anything."

42

"Such was the union that came to Astarte. This was accomplished by splitting herself into two, giving herself the perfect partner that she so desired to share with, her soul twin, for he was a part of her own soul. Astarte herself retained the more feminine and more compassionate side of her own nature."

"You are her offspring in this world. She was pure light, while the other half, the newly created soul, was given the more masculine and darker side. This soul's name was Mahade, and the cowboy is his offspring in this world."

"Now, these two souls always had a choice. They could pursue their lessons separately, as individual souls, and still be considered as one, for even when far away from each other, they could still feel and draw strength from the very existence of the other, reuniting from time to time, or, they could stand together, side by side, never being apart throughout eternity."

"There was only one choice for Astarte and Mahade. They could not endure being apart and upon separation, their agony and their pain was felt throughout the entire universe. They wanted to be together eternally. They asked God if they could merge together in an inseparable union, which is the highest form of marriage in the superior realms, for each becomes one with the other forever, bonded into the same being, even though still distinct and individual in their own way. Because of their unyielding devotion and great love for each other their wish was granted. They were then entered into a permanent soul partnership and marriage for all time by the hand of God. Separate their heart was broken, while together their heart is healed, and in service to God and the highest good."

"Now, Astarte and Mahade have many offspring, who are represented by the leaves on their great tree. A master soul, such as they, has many lessons to learn and many to teach, in its pursuit of spiritual perfection, and because of this, it is the source or parents of more than one offspring, which enables it to experience and to assimilate many different lessons at the same time."

"A master soul can be in several different dimensions and times at once, which greatly accelerates its growth. A soul knows that all time is one, and that linear time, which is one event happening in succession after the other, is but a convenient illusion created by man using limited third dimensional thinking for his simplified understanding."

"A master soul is not restricted by third dimensional thinking, but is, in fact, in all dimensions at the same time. Therefore, it has many offspring living, learning and teaching in many different dimensions and at many different times simultaneously. You and the cowboy have many distant relatives living in different dimensions of reality at different times at this moment."

"The dimensions of reality, and the many living worlds contained within those dimensions are limitless. A master soul can support their offspring in these various dimensions with ease, while incorporating their knowledge and experiences into its core, which is the trunk of the tree. As the leaves of the tree symbolize the offspring, or personalities, the branches are the various soul families supporting these offspring in the different dimensions and times."

"You, the channel, and he, the cowboy, are the only children of Astarte and Mahade living in this world. As your parents before you, you were meant to be together. You both may, or may not choose to be physically together in this lifetime, even though you are already spiritually one, for as I have said before, God's gift to his children is that of free will. But, for countless lifetimes, you have both followed in the footsteps of your parents, which is why you met again in this lifetime. When separated from each other, your mutual pain echoes throughout the universe, and you search until you find each other. Reunited, you are happy and complete again. Only true love and the unwillingness to part from each other can complete the cycle."

So it was that they met, coming together from different sides of the country, to be joined as one. Their souls had an agreement which was rare and unusual even on universal terms, that they would always stand together no matter what the circumstances, for they could not endure separation. The differences in their personalities or their lives did not matter to them, for the pain of being separate was too much for them to bear. They were living a deeper birthright that superceded any physical incarnation, and were only continuing a legacy that had existed since the beginning of time. They had an immortal love which never died.

She flew back and forth like a bird with two nests, caring for her family in the east, and caring for him in the west. She could be physically in Pennsylvania, but she was always with him in her heart. And it was the same for him, as he rode the trails of his mountains, for he was always thinking of her and her gentle ways.

Matheu watched them both, bringing words of encouragement to the girl, while sending dreams of peace and safety to the boy through his own guides, as he slept missing her.

So the towering forests and the lush green fields of Pennsylvania, became one with the rugged desert and the rocky mountains of Arizona, as their souls united them both, and for these two children, the world itself became like a giant cradle, rocking them together with unseen hands.

She came from privilege and a family heritage that echoed of that privilege. He had no legacy, and lived in a small room over a stable. Yet, she never knew true wealth until she shared that room with him. There, she felt rich beyond her wildest dreams, for in that palace of a room they were not commoners of this world, but royalty of their own kingdom.

It was a cowboy's room, that reflected who he was, to which she added touches of her own gentle nature to make it even more comfortable and a part of them both. When she stepped in that room, her whole life faded in the essence of his personality, and it was like coming home for the first time.

They had a small handmade wooden bed, just barely big enough for two to sleep side by side, which she covered with the softest quilt she could find. Two worn chairs circled a braided rug around an old television set he had bought. She brought an old VCR from Pennsylvania, and most nights you could find them seated around the TV, with his flaxen haired German Shepherd, Sheba, lying quietly in the corner, intent on their every move. Sheba seemed to be a part of him, for she obeyed his every order, and could almost read his mind before he spoke. Over time, she had come to love Joy as much as he did, and greeted her with a frenzied welcome fit for the mistress of the castle, rather than the ferocity she saved for a stranger. The three of them watched every cowboy movie ever made, lost in their own world. Their favorite was Larry McMurtry's <u>Lonesome Dove</u>, for it seemed to mimic his lifestyle exactly, only he was real.

The walls of the room were covered with western paraphanalia. Bridles with bits that sparkled like silver and gold hung everywhere, with their long hand braided reins hanging down the walls like Rapunzel's hair. His saddle stood in the corner on an old saddle rack, with a horseshoe nailed in front for good luck. A Winchester rifle hung over the door, near his gunbelt, which held his loaded 22 revolver. Hanging between the western gear, were elusive pieces to the puzzle of his personality. They were the pen and ink drawings that he had done on lonely nights of the old West, showing the depth of his talent as an artist. His finely tooled leatherwork hung in various places. Saddlebags, canteens, spur straps and spurs, of all shapes and sizes, each bearing his mark, decorated the room, creating a panoramic feast for the eye to behold. All of this reflected his creativity and the pioneer spirit which he cherished so deeply.

She built a tiny kitchen in the corner of the room with a hotplate and a small refrigerator, so they had all the comforts of home right there, and they rarely left the room to socialize, but preferred to stay alone with just each other and Sheba for company.

Socialization came with his job and they were grateful for the times they could be alone, away from the gawking tourists. Their only passion was riding together in the mountains, either by themselves, or when he was escorting others as a guide. At those times, she rode quietly beside him and she knew that even when he was speaking to them, his eyes were on her, watching her every move.

Sometimes at night, when the busy day was done, they would sit outside together and watch the millions of stars that seemed close enough to touch, not speaking, but basking in each other's company. She would smile secretly at the heavens, which were home to her many friends, and they would smile back, seeing their children happy and at peace. What they had to others did not seem like much, but it was more than anything could ever be.

She knew of his pain, and though they didn't speak of it often, she could feel it oozing into her skin like salty tears, especially when he would withdraw into his shell and drink, almost forgetting that she was there. At those times she would try to leave him alone, and focus on her own thoughts, as he drowned in his and in the bottle. She wanted to stop him from drinking and to heal his pain. But she knew in her heart that only he could heal himself. So she stood quietly by, ready to protect and support him, feeling his agony and guilt for crimes of the heart which he did not commit, but for which he punished himself. All she could do at those times of terror was to be there, accepting him for who he was, and loving him unconditionally as she had been taught by the guides, who in their turn had been taught by God himself. So she passed that great legacy of love and acceptance down to him, accepting him no matter what, as spirit had accepted her, and she never left his side.

At times they would speak of God and spirit, but he didn't seem to believe, so she left it silent mostly, knowing that he had to learn on his own. She knew that he had an enormous amount of healing to do, and this was but the first step on a very long road for him in healing his heart.

So she didn't preach, and he didn't question, because for both of them, it was enough that they were together. She knew that through his faith in their love, though he didn't speak of it, a greater faith might find its way into his heart, so talking was unnecessary. Everyone knows words are inadequate, for love must be felt instead of spoken.

All she did was be herself and though he didn't know it, through her love, he felt God's love and the love of the guides mingling with her own, passed through her to him in simple ways.

He could not believe the feeling of safety he experienced when he was with her. He had never been comfortable anywhere, but if she were there, he felt complete. It was as if she were a part of him, like Sheba. He could just be himself, and she would accept him as he was without any moral judgement. He didn't

47

think of it in terms of love, for it was more than that. Without her he felt as if a part of him was missing, and it was no more necessary to talk about that part than it was for his lungs to acknowledge the air that they breathed. She was just necessary to his existence, and he was afraid when she was gone.

He had never experienced this feeling before, and at first, he didn't like it. He thought a lot about it, more than he expressed to her, but she already knew, for she was feeling the same way. It felt as if he were being controlled or owned, but she never did anything to control him. She was sweet and unassuming, and it was her very innocence that frightened him. It was obvious that she trusted him. Nobody had ever believed in him like this before. It was not her actions or her words that gave her power, it was her presence that was so overwhelming, for he knew that she was the only thing that had ever given him any hope in himself.

At times he tried to fight it, and he would withhold his love by being silent, but he still needed her, and wouldn't let her go. At those times he only wound up hurting himself. His mind would become enemies with his heart and soul. "I don't believe in anyone or anything," he would say to himself in a bad moment. But his heart and his soul told him differently, and at those dark times he thought he would die of emptiness if she left him.

The only time she was ever afraid was when he drank, and would become so drunk he would sink into the black hole of his past, and not she, nor the heavens could reach him. The alcohol was too strong, and the darkness too deep. It was then that he succumbed to the demons of his pain, and tried to anesthetize them through the fire water.

Most of the time when he was drinking, he remained passive and withdrawn in his own inner world. At other times he became more aggressive, and the rage within him threatened to explode the surface of his personality. Then he would seem possessed of a darker nature, almost to the point of becoming someone different, and later on would have no memory of what he had said or what he had done. Life became an out of blur focus to him as his drunken mind hallucinated, merging past, present and future into one tormented nightmare, from which he could not awaken or control, until the devil of the drink had tired of him, and left him until the next time.

One night after a massive drinking binge of tequila, beer and whiskey chasers, he was still standing, but his mind was destroyed and he did not recognize her or Sheba. His personality changed, and he became very angry. It was as if something darker and much more sinister had eclipsed the light of who he was, and he became a total stranger. He started to curse and mutter strange phrases to her, "Why did you leave me... women are nothing but whores."

She had managed to get him home from the bar, and they were standing in their stable room. He stumbled over to his gunbelt, and drew his loaded 22 from its holster. He pointed it at her, threatening to kill her, or whoever he thought she was.

Time moved in slow motion as she stood there frozen with fear, facing down the barrel of his gun, in the hands of the man that she loved, who suddenly seemed possessed by a demon. Her body couldn't move, but her mind was clear, for she never drank. All of a sudden she felt Matheu's warmth surround her, and heard him softly say, "Don't panic little one, he is not going to shoot you. Talk softly to him and remind him of who you are."

With the sound of the great guide's voice, her courage returned, so she took a deep breath and started to whisper to him who she was and that she would never leave him, all the while walking forward into the barrel of the gun, drawing him back from the darkness into the light of her love.

There was an animal of hatred inside of him that did not want to hear or feel or think about anything. It wanted to consume and be consumed by the hatred's fire. Out of the darkness it had come, and it wanted to stay and remain in control.

Here was a challenge for it, for it was facing one of His. It had been drawn as much by her, as by the bitter boy and his drinking. The boy's anger and intoxication had only provided the avenue and the vehicle for its presence. But it was not after the boy. It was after her. It had been drawn by her light and it wanted to extinguish it. It had never had an opportunity to get to her until now. She was protected by them, but he was not. His soul was darker, and the alcohol had weakened him, making him vulnerable to predators. She was a channel of their light, and he could have her in an instant, extinguishing that light, and wounding the heart of Christ through her.

Somewhere inside of the cowboy, he heard her voice and it reminded him of the feelings of peace and love that he had felt when she came into his life. He struggled within himself to get control of his mind, against the burning hatred that was trying to overpower him, which seemed to know everything about him and was using that knowledge against him.

She continued walking towards him, speaking softly, and he began to back up, still holding the gun pointed towards her, watching her every move, until he was backed up against the bed. She slowly put out her hand to stroke his which held the weapon, and at that gentle touch, he lowered the gun, and fell back on the mattress as if something had struck him. He started to cry and climbing on the bed next to him, she held him soothingly, not saying a word until he finally passed out from exhaustion.

She carefully got up so as not to awaken him and put the gun away, where he would not be able to find it, still shaken by what had happened. She had sensed something beside Matheu and them in the room, but she didn't know what it was. The guides told her to go to sleep, that the danger had passed and she would be safe. They told her they would explain later when she was in a better state of mind.

So she laid down, suddenly very tired, grateful that he was there lying next to her, for she had almost lost him to something that she had felt, but did not understand. She was comforted by the strong presence of the guides in the room, guarding them, and cradling them both to sleep.

He woke up the next morning as if nothing had happened. She watched him silently as he got dressed for work, amazed that he showed no signs of remembering the horror of the night before. After dressing, he went to get his gun, which was part of his gear for riding in the mountains. It wasn't there. "Where is my gun?" he asked, clearly puzzled.

She went to the closet and pulled it out from behind some boxes where it had been hidden, and handed it to him.

"Why did you put it there?" he asked. She explained what had happened.

He felt as if he had been kicked in the chest by a horse. He couldn't breathe. His face became the window of his emotions, as he turned blood red, then ashen white. He struggled in his mind blindly for the memory of the night before, but he could only remember leaving the bar and nothing more. Everything after that was black, as if time had stopped and he with it, only to restart that very morning with the rising of the sun.

He didn't know what to say. Apologies didn't seem to be enough. His shame, mixed with the horror of what might have happened had he not been stopped, overcame him.

Panicked, he told her he would never hurt her again, and that it was the pain from his past, which had plagued him his whole life, leading him to drink. He confessed that he didn't know how to control either, and that it had always been that way. He was terrified of losing her, now that she knew the truth about him.

Forgiveness is easy, when you truly love someone. In that instant she forgave him everything, despite what had happened. She had not forgotten the darkness in him, but she understood it, accepted it, and embraced it as a part of loving him for who he was. Neither of them could even imagine a world without each other, no matter what it brought them.

Nothing had changed between them, except a growing awareness that they belonged together. She now had experienced the anger in him, and the dangerous darkness that accompanied it, but it made no difference to her, for she could see beyond it into the truth of his heart. She loved that heart more than she feared death.

He, too, had learned something. He now knew of the light within her, and the love within that light that held an enormous capacity for forgiveness. With that came the revelation that she had seen him at his worst and despite that had not judged him, but had embraced him wholly and unconditionally, loving him as before. This was his first glimpse of the unconditional love that he was denied as a child. He would rather die than hurt her.

This was an important moment for them both, for they had made a choice. Because of their total acceptance of each other, they became inseperable from that moment on.

Upon returning to Pennsylvania to be with her children, she and Matheu spoke about what had happened.

"Little one, he is your oldest companion in time. You have been together through countless lifetimes and will continue to be together long after this lifetime is over. This, however, is perhaps the most important lifetime of them all, for it is the culmination of all that has gone on before, and may result in the oneness that you both so desperately seek from each other in the future. It is the next step in your growth. But he, as well as you, my dearest Astarte, must choose this, based upon the truth of your hearts. I cannot choose it for you, but can only advise you with my knowledge and my love for you. Oneness can only be attained through unconditional love, and the total acceptance of that which comes from it. The desire cannot be forced or falsified, but must evolve genuinely."

"If you both so wanted, you could temporarily end this relationship during this lifetime, using your own free will, which is your right. You could do this based upon his anger and related behavior, which will continue, and he could do it based upon his fear of giving and receiving love, which will continue to haunt him, thereby perpetuating the anger and the negative behavior. This in itself, would be a difficult choice for you both to make, for it is a certainty that you would miss each other greatly, and both of you would always feel as if someone or something was missing from your lives. As your soul parents before you, you are a part of each other. It would feel like losing a part of yourselves. But still, it could be done, and your physical realities would go on as before you met, only they would seem more meaningless."

"If you choose to end this, then you would meet him again after this lifetime is over, after both of you have traveled independently of each other for this brief time, to be reunited once again at the soul level. Then you would begin again. There would be no judgement on this decision, for there is no right or wrong decision in the universe, only actions which determine the course and the timing of one's growth. But make no mistake, all decisions eventually lead to the same place. In the universe you can run, but you cannot hide, for the lesson of unconditional love will be learned in one way or another, sooner or later, when you are both ready for it."

"The other alternative is to stay together, knowing that if you do, the road is extremely dark and dangerous due to his drinking and his inner anger. On that road you will have only your faith and your love to guide you. It is the same for him as it is for you, for in choosing love, he chooses to face this anger and to overcome it. He must learn not to fear love, but to trust it, knowing that true love will not leave him as his mother did. That is his healing, and together, ultimately yours."

"During this lifetime, the cowboy has many lessons to learn about the dark side of his soul, and the effect it has on the whole of him. In essence, he must restore his faith in God and the unconditional love that faith brings, even in the darkest of times, so that he can become complete within himself."

"You will also be tested, for you must maintain your great faith during the worst of it, for faith that is strong only during the good times, but which fades during the bad times, is not really faith at all, but only an illusion of a greater faith. Your light must burn as bright in your darkest hour as in your shining moments, knowing that God will never abandon you."

"As different as you appear to be on the surface, you are both similar in your fears of abandonment. God will never abandon you, as you well know, and true love, as God's love is true, cannot be lost. It just isn't possible, for true love brings a union of spirit which lasts forever.

"This is something you have already experienced through your channeling, and you know it well. This is our credo and our service. But you cannot teach him through words, for he must be shown through deeds, and in doing so you will be tested to the limits of your endurance. His anger makes him an unwilling pupil, for he is afraid to learn to love again. But love cannot be taught, only felt, and must learned through experience. You are a shining example of that higher love. But he must see it for himself and embrace it on his own. Neither God, nor *I*, nor you, has any right to force this on him. It is his choice to learn in his own time. If this happens, and it may take a very long time for his wounds are very deep, then he will be healed."

"Now, he has the path of an alcoholic in this lifetime. This path was chosen with him and for him, by God and his soul before his birth. You have the opposite path. You were born a channel and a healer. This path was also chosen with you and for you, by God and your soul before you were born. You must get beyond the illusion and the fear of this reality to find the truth of who you really are. You must live your faith. It is only by accepting that truth that you can find the greater love within and enter into a lasting relationship."

"He may or may not heal in this lifetime. It make take longer. He has not chosen yet, nor have you. But if he does not heal in this lifetime, it will become a dangerous journey into darkness, which could physically destroy you both. This is something which you have already seen."

"His parents have abandoned him, society has shunned him, and you will be joining him on that road. Do you love him enough to stay with him knowing that it may worsen before it gets better? Will you stay with him knowing that he may not heal in this lifetime, for the damage to him is very severe, and this lesson of unconditional love may extend beyond the boundaries of this physical reality into the next? Will you stand by his side knowing that you may sacrifice your own physical well being in this world? Will you walk with him into an alcoholic hell, facing poverty and destruction, a living example of faith in the God that you have chosen to serve? Will you risk all that you have to hold a candle for him on his journey into darkness? These are the questions you must answer for yourself."

"He also has a difficult choice to make. Will he stand by your side facing his greatest fear? For to him, to love is to die, as he was taught so long ago at his mother's knee."

"If you do, there will be times when you will question your own faith, and what you have learned. You will face terror, fear, and ultimately temptation to go in another direction. You will risk all in order to live your belief. Your resources will be drained by the alcoholism, and you will be constantly tested by it. You will be exposed to the dark side of life, which is very different from what you already know. I will guide you as best I can, but you yourself must walk the path. Most people will shun you, for they will not understand what you are doing. They will only see what is before their eyes, which will be alcoholism and the destruction that it brings. They will not see the truth of the higher road. You will be judged, and judged harshly. At best, you will be left with a handful of friends, and they will only be those who share your unique ability to see beyond the physical world and its illusions. But I will tell you that this test of courage is the highest path for you both, even though at times, it may seem like just the opposite. This may lead you to a greater love than you have ever thought possible, that will symbolize God's unconditional love for all his children. You must decide for yourselves, if you will follow the path of the heart."

The cowboy sat in Arizona, tormented by what had happened. More and more when he drank, the anger and the pain of the past spilled from him like a cup overflowing. He could not seem to control the river rising in him. These emotions had been dammed up for so long they threatened to burst. Because of her, the feelings had started to leak out. It was as if she had reached into the deepest part of him, to touch those hidden places which had not been touched since he was a child. At times, he was pulled down into the drunken vortex of that dark water, like he was drowning, and he would hear strange voices and lose consciousness, giving control to whatever was haunting him. Now, his thoughts were always with her and what might be. What if he had pulled the trigger? He was afraid of what would happen between them if they stayed together, but he was more afraid of letting her go. In his heart he knew she was the only thing worth living or dying for. The fear of losing her was so great, that he needed a drink to relieve it. He vowed to make it up to her when she came back home to him.

She sat back in her chair, her thoughts echoing with Matheu's words. She had heard everything that he said, and the warnings contained within. For a moment, her mind became confused and afraid, but her heart was steady, and told her something completely different. Without hesitation, she softly answered him.

"Matheu, I must follow my heart. That is what led me to you. Whether it leads to Heaven or Hell I am going with him. I choose the path of the heart."

Then they sat silent for a time, the old guide holding her softly as silent tears streamed down her cheeks, like a river of sorrow for the boy's pain, which she could not erase.

Matheu sighed in resignation. The lesson had begun, and though the children did not understand it, they were part of an even greater battle that was forming on the earth. The world itself was entering into a period of change in which its future would be decided. Individuals, such as she, were beginning to elevate their energy to a higher frequency in preparation. Assistance, such as he, was being provided on all levels. A series of astrological events would form tidal waves of energy washing the shores of the earth. Through their force, they would create corresponding physical and psychic changes on the planet, resulting in a new environment which would assist mankind with its growth. This was not a gentle energy, but a fierce one that would wash away the old stagnant energy that was holding people back, allowing a new and higher, more vibrant energy to take its place. There would be some destruction, but out of it would be the creation of a new beginning.

This would be a lengthy process, forcing people from their protective shells of fear and isolation into faith and unity. Mankind would begin to realize that he was multidimensional, and the world itself would rise from the ashes of limited third dimensional thinking into the phoenix of fifth dimensional reality. The lid was being taken off the box, and people would begin to see they were not alone in the universe.

All life would come full circle, united under God. This was not the mythology of God which the world had created, but his true essence coming into being.

There would be a great battle of two forces, which would ultimately result in mankind's destiny. The battle of good versus evil, which had been simmering since the beginning of time was beginning to escalate and boil towards a final and ultimate resolution. They had been chosen, as so many others before them, to set an example for the rest of the world. Their love did not just represent limited mortal love, but eternal love, for all are born of the light and unconditionally loved by God, though they are not always recognized for who they are.

He thought of the girl in prior incarnations and how he had shielded her from them. He had kept her so busy in the present, that she had shown no real interest in them. This had been necessary so that her faith could be reborn from a fresh perspective, making it stronger. Deep roots are nothing if they do not sprout fresh growth, and old faith was nothing but a foundation from which a newer and stronger faith could spring. Each personality was a newborn, washed clean, and carrying but a sleeping memory of its complete soul ancestry. Everyone came into the world untarnished, and ready to begin anew. He knew the time was coming when she would seek more answers, but it was not now. Her burden in the present would be heavy enough. But the souls of Astarte and Mahade had walked this way of faith many times over, before these children were even born.

He vowed to protect them both, for he loved his protege, and through her, he loved the boy as his own. They had made their choice freely, and through that choice, they had chosen God and the faith of Christ. They were honoring the light within all living things, which knew that through God and unconditional love, all things are possible.

Time stood still as she waited for him to continue. He seemed preoccupied with his own thoughts, but she sensed in his silence that he was not finished with what he had to say to her, but was only searching for the right way to say it.

She had questions to ask of him already forming in her mind, but she sat patiently until he was ready to begin again, just enjoying the warmth of his loving energy. There was no rushing Matheu. Then he spoke once more, as if reading her mind.

"You are about to embark on a new journey in your life. Many things will change. You will become of a partnership, that will effect the entirety of who you are today. Wherever that road may lead you, I will be there with the love and support that I have always given you. Though other things may change, that

57

will never change. You have grown since we first established our relationship, and I feel very much as a mortal father might feel, when he has raised a daughter from childhood to adulthood. You, my daughter, are about to leave the protected nest. You will feel more on your own than you have ever felt. But always remember, you are never alone, for my heart will be your home wherever you may travel, and you may always find rest within my love for you."

"You will see that your experiences have made you different from most. This is both a blessing and a curse. At times, it will be a comfort to know what lies beyond the mortal world and at other times it will cause you great fear and pain, because it will isolate you from all but your peers."

"When this happens remember who you are, dear one. This will help you on your path. Your ability to channel comes from your soul, which is very old. It is much older than the young woman I see before me with the lovesick eyes. It is the seat of your power, and can be compared to a modern day battery from which you draw your strength. Its power, for all purposes in this lifetime is limitless. You could never drain it. You and only you, are that soul in this dimension, and drawing on its energy. Others on this planet have their own souls which they are a part of, and whose strength they may draw upon. Always go within to use that power which you are so entitled to. It will protect you more than you may know, and it will give you all the strength that you will need."

"Your soul's strength comes from its age and level of achievement. Its stature reaches to the angelic realm. This level is just below Christ and his companion souls. Beyond Christ is the level of perfection, or the Source of All Things, which you know as God. Below your soul's level are various dimensions, or states of being, which progressively lead to that state of perfection. These levels are the Buddiac, the Causal, and the Astral planes. Each plane has many levels and living worlds contained within it."

"Imagine a funnel upside down, with the broad base being at the bottom, and the narrow circumferance being at the top. Now imagine this funnel collapsing, or folding down within itself. All

58

time and space become one. The earthbound existence forms the wide base, with God emerging at the very narrow top as the pinnacle. All souls are multidimensional, stretching through that funnel and through the many dimensions between, in many living worlds at the same time, but not all souls reach to that stature or level, which is almost to the top of that funnel. That is dependent on their age, their experience, and very importantly, how hard they have worked at their spiritual growth, either during an incarnation or between them. Some souls, as some people, work harder than others. Some souls being much younger, need more time to grow. Only God knows all the reasons for a soul's level of growth, for only God, who is the Source of All Things, can incorporate all knowledge into wisdom and truth. Therefore, only God may judge another. Your soul has earned its level of worth through much hard work and devotion to God. It has made many sacrifices for its faith. But it never judges another, for only God has that right."

"That is why, when you channel, you receive answers from the highest possible sources. Those souls that are more evolved than yours have no questions and need no answers, for they are just one with the heart of God. Others who channel may receive answers from equal or lower sources, depending on their own soul's level of growth. At this level the work is harder and the demand for perfection greater. This is also why on your journey you will find very few who truly understand you. There will be some. But the majority of souls are not of your growth, so the majority of people you meet will be concerned with what will appear to be almost trivial matters."

"A good example of this are the psychic lines, which deal with matters of reality, such as who will I meet, where will I work, and what will my physical reality be like. The answers to these questions to a younger soul will seem of paramount importance, for they cannot see beyond the physical level of growth. They wish to avoid taking responsibility for the creation of their own lives. They have limited vision and limited ability, and therefore will receive limited answers. You and your equals will be more concerned with the soul's level of growth and its effect on the illusion of the living world. This is in opposition to the younger soul, who will focus on the living world as the source of all reality. You know it is exactly the opposite, for the physical world is an illusion created by God for the soul's education and evolution. The soul level is the reality, which transcends all illusions. You can move from dimension to dimension, living world to living world, changing the illusion, but you would find the circumstances to be the same and you would wind up in a similar position, until you change and grow inside. Know that what you are facing in your life is the next step and is necessary to your overall growth."

"It is not enough to have a strong soul. Many have strong souls who are full of wisdom, and ready to help them in their time of need. Souls are always eager to be drawn upon, much as a parent is willing and eager to help a child whose growth is in progress, but not many utilize the strength of their souls. Creation always comes from the soul level, not from the physical level. But in order to achieve this, one must be intent on becoming one with their soul, acknowledging its existence, and learning to rely upon it, but few are willing to do that, because it takes focus and hard work. One must be willing to leave the physical reality behind, and to view life from a different and higher perspective. Everyday life and its petty problems become an absurdity when you look at things from the higher perspective, for in essence you will find yourself forced to do menial and trivial things, when you can already see beyond them. Much of the world's problems could be solved should they be viewed from the higher perspective. Such is the difference between the eagle and the ant. One toils carrying bits and pieces of their survival, while the other flies freely above that, carried by life itself."

"You have worked very hard at becoming one with your soul and its purpose. You have sat on the higher levels with your guides. This is partly due to your soul's purpose in this lifetime, which is so strong, it has allowed the physical circumstances of your existence to free you to do your work, but, it is also due to the level of hard work and devotion you have shown to your growth. It is to your credit, for it has always been your choice to do this, for the years you have spent in school with me and other guides, could well have been spent in more pleasurable earthbound activities."

"I am a difficult and a demanding teacher, but you are an excellent student. You have undergone many physical changes to accomplish this, sometimes, to your discomfort. You have been cellularly restructured to handle the higher energy current. It has not been easy for you. But you have never quit, no matter what the pain physically or emotionally, and for this I commend you. Regardless of what the world may think of you, remember, we, who truly know you, are very proud of you."

"At times, you will feel lonely in the physical world, for not many will have shared your spiritual experiences. There are not many who are willing to divorce themselves from the satisfaction of a physical existence for the higher path. They may ask for help in getting started, perhaps they will start to meditate in hopes of connecting with their guides or higher self, but then, more often than not, they will quit when they find it involves intense discipline and hard work. They will go off and resume their normal earthbound activities. When they need help, they will call a psychic for they are not ready for the truth about themselves."

"But you are one of a select few who have put your growth first and your pleasure later. I can truly say that you are not of the physical dimensions anymore, but have spent so much time in the ethers of the higher realities, that your energy has been permanently altered. Your energy remains, and always will, in the higher dimensions of thought and creation, even if the world sometimes contains painful earthbound experiences for you."

"Be of the eagle, instead of the ant. Do not live the illusion anymore, but the truth, and though you may fear it at times, you will never be lost, for you will be guided from within by the strength of your soul in its work to your destiny."

"This journey that you undertake in your life is far more important than you already know, and also far more difficult. But that is the level of growth that you are at. Be a pathmaker, instead of a pathfollower, for the work you do, you do for everyone, that the ants someday may become eagles themselves, and know the joy of becoming one with the wind of life.

Remember your faith in times of trouble, and that true faith overcomes all obstacles in God's time. You have already learned that nothing is impossible. Do not believe in what you see with your eyes, or hear with your ears. That may well be an illusion. Look beyond those illusions into the truth of every situation. Believe in what you know to be true, not what appears to be true."

"I know it has been a labor of love for you, and that you have not done this out of curiousity, or seeking power, but because you truly love God and his brethren. Otherwise my dear, the path would have been blocked, as it has been for so many others, for only those that come of their hearts, in faith and humility, are shown the way. Those that come on a whim, or in greed, or seeking dominance over others, remain at a lower vibration until they learn the lesson of love and selflessness."

"This is your legacy from your soul, the legacy of unconditional love. That is why you are called Astarte, which is a name in universal terms meaning love of others. You will meet others who seek their soul names, but they are unwilling to labor for them as you have. This knowledge and this inheritance must be earned by the individual, by becoming one with their soul. Do you remember the day I first called you by your soul name? You argued with me that you were not worthy of it. I remember we settled the argument by agreeing that you were Astarte's big toe, and nothing more. Then, and only then would you allow me to call you by that name. It is your rightful name, and you have earned it. To me, you are more her heart, than her foot. Use that name in your work, for it is a name of great honor, which you have earned."

"Do not look for answers from your past lives. Along your journey you will meet many who will seek answers for today's problems from their past lifetimes. They will be consumed with the fact that they might have been someone of great importance, to compensate for what they feel is lacking within themselves today. Those who cannot handle today, will not find the answer in yesterday or even in tomorrow. They must find themselves in the present, before they can even begin to understand the past or the future. It is that simple. There are no answers in reincarnation or in psychic prediction, All is predicated upon understanding yourself in the present. It is from the moment that truth and reality are created, not from the past or the future."

"You do not ask about previous incarnations, nor do I offer such information at this time for one reason. Each personality, though it may carry ancestral traits from prior incarnations, stands on its own in God's eyes, and each has new meaning and purpose. One cannot rest upon one's past laurels, but must start fresh in each lifetime in order to truly achieve growth. For faith to be true, it must not be founded on history, but fresh from the heart and in the moment. It does not matter who you were, that is poppycock, but who you are right now. The soul of Astarte, of which you are but a part of, has been many places in its growth, but you need not concern yourself with them now."

"Indeed, the same can be said for the future, for destiny is not guaranteed, but must be earned and created one moment at a time. Those who usually ask such questions are not very evolved in their growth and are looking for a quick route to the top. There is no quick route, only slow growth through evolutionary lifetimes of hard work."

"Mankind may be suprised to find that the homeless person on their street corner is one of great stature on the soul level, who has taken on the posture of selflessness to teach and to learn a great lesson on the physical plane, while the royalty of many nations are but fledging souls still learning to walk. The appearance of success can be very deceptive. Look within a person, not without for true recognition."

"In innocence you will find your strength. There may come a time when you will learn more about past lives with your cowboy, but they are unimportant right now. They are over, and this one is not, and you must never let the thought of them interfere with who you are today, The same could be said for your future. Looking ahead too much denies you the power of creation in the present. Never lose touch with your heart in the moment, for it is indeed a beautiful one, and he is a very lucky man. That you two were together in many lifetimes is not of true importance. That you were meant to be together is also not important. That must be earned in the moment over time. Look

63

within your heart today for that is how life is created. Joy loves JJ and JJ loves Joy, and those other past or future lives can add nothing to what is already a shining truth on its own."

"As you counsel others, you may feel overwhelmed by people seeking answers to trivial questions about their future. Don't get entangled in the illusion of prophecy. You are good at it, and at times you may choose to utilize that ability, but remember to stay grounded in the present. The future is created in the moment, and through that creation, certain outcomes may be changed making all predictions moot."

"As one of your radios transmits a signal to reach the surrounding area, so do you as a channel transmit at a higher frequency. This frequency is in the range of spirit and other channels who are also at a similar vibration. A simplistic example of this are dogs. Only they can hear the high pitched whistle calling them, for they are naturally in tune to it, while others will hear nothing. People who are at a lower vibration are like untuned instruments. They will be unable to hear this higher sound. Due to a combination of elements, such as your soul, your hard work with the light, not to mention my own training, you put out a strong signal. Because of this, your experiences have been greater than the norm. Do not expect everyone who has some psychic ability to have experienced what you have experienced, for not everyone has all of these same elements in the right combination. Many have some awareness of spirit, but few have been raised by them."

"You will meet those along the way who are trying desperately to manifest what they desire in life. They do not know how to create what they may desire, so they are trying to control what they want through manipulation and power. There is a great difference between the power of creation and that of control. One brings to you what you may truly need through a soundness of self within the flow of life, while the other is a form of thievery which only brings negative results and a dearth of satisfaction. Those that obcessively try to control the greater flow will not be successful. There are many fradulent teachers who indoctrinate their students with their teachings of power. They are passing down this legacy of control. They will teach them that through rituals of power they can get whatever they want. They cannot get beyond their own egos into the truth of the matter. One does not create through force, but by letting go, and becoming one with the greater flow, allowing it to bring to you what you may need for your greatest good. It will not help their cause, for they are only obstructing their own path and that of their soul. I say to you, let things happen naturally."

"Preoccupation with destiny only serves to hold one back, denying one's dreams. Trust in the flow, for you cannot master what is greater than you, but can only become a part of it, allowing it to bring to you what you may need and deserve in your growth for your life. The greater flow is not there to serve you, but for you to serve it. Nothing external is necessary. Remember, prayer is a form of mastery."

"Some will weigh and measure every word, thought and action. They believe that they will become better souls if they are careful about what they say, feel and do. They restrict themselves and by doing so, they create their own obstacles and their own pain. They limit their own growth. Actions and emotions must also be a part of the greater flow. Be natural. You are in human form for a reason."

"It is only by experiencing these feelings that one learns how to deal with them. It is necessary to express them at times, for in doing so you validate yourself and the lesson which needs to be learned by you or another."

"By suppressing these feelings you create blocks, ultimately postponing the lesson and the resolution. You impede the flow. This creates obstacles in your growth and that of others, instead of removing them. There is no karma created by being true to yourself, and by expressing that truth. It is only when you go against the truth and the natural process that karma is created."

"Let me give you an example. If someone intentionally injures your child, you become angry. That anger is justified. By releasing that anger in proportion to the deed, the person who created the injury learns the lesson that it is wrong to hurt another. The child feels validated through your protection. And you yourself serve justice where it needs to be served. By releasing that natural emotion, it serves the purpose that it is meant to serve, then it dissipates. It fades away over time. If suppressed, it blocks the lessons, and the suppressed anger grows larger within and begins to fester. The soul becomes troubled and may act out that anger at a later date in an unproportionate manner. That is when problems begin and horrible things happen. By releasing that initial anger there is no karma. By containing it, you create karma, for your suppression has long ranging effects you cannot see at the time, on yourself and on others."

"Perhaps the person that hurt the child, having not received their lesson because of your suppression, will go out and create a greater hurt. That is your karma. Perhaps the child will grow up feeling unprotected and unloved. He, in turn, will pass that feeling down to his own children. That also is your karma. As long as the feeling is proportionate with the deed, then balance is maintained and justice is served. By negating your emotions, they become engorged and out of proportion. You have never had a problem with expressing your feelings, as I well know, and this has made you stronger in the greater flow."

"Remember that spiritual growth is not a business. It is a natural state of being, like breathing, and cannot be obtained through outside sources. You cannot find it in a specific church. It may be in all or none, depending upon the individuals who are worshipping there. It cannot be found in a deck of Tarot cards. It comes from the heart and can only be experienced in your own way. Essentially, it lies between the individual and his Creator, and is a natural process, like birth or death. You have always done what you thought was right, even though you may have had information from us to the contrary. This is why you have been allowed to receive more information than most about your life. You use it properly by thinking for yourself. The road you choose must be your own, for you will always get to where you are going, one way or another, when you are ready for it."

"You will meet those along the way who are charging a great deal of money to teach spiritual growth. They will tell the innocent that to be spiritual they must do or believe in certain things. This is not true. To be spiritual one must not be afraid to be themselves, whatever that might be, true to their own nature and to their God who created them that way. As you well know, one must only take a bath, or a walk, or listen to music, one must only find their own hearts, and be happy within them, trusting to that greater flow that will take them home. One must surrender. To truly help another, one must show them the way to help themselves through developing a faith of their own."

"Do not listen to anyone and when in doubt, look within. I am there, God is there, and so is your cowboy, for all are one. If you do this, no matter what you choose, you will always walk with God on the path of the heart."

"You will continue, as usual, to attract a great many guides and visitors from other dimensions. Some of them you already know, and some, you have yet to meet. But I must warn you that there are entities that are not of the light, but of the darkness, who are also aware of your presence."

"I have done all that I can to protect you in your growth. For all your experiences, you have led a quiet and unassuming life establishing your abilities within the light. Yet, you have experienced the darker side. Do you remember that evening when you went to a bookstore and encountered the darker forces?" he asked.

"I was followed by a man there who touched my hand. He said he was attracted to me," she replied.

"That man had a very dark soul, for he dabbled in the occult trying to control his destiny and that of others. He was attracted to you because of your bright energy. When he touched your hand, discarnate entities who followed him, attached themselves to you from his being. These entities were nothing but deceased and negative people stuck in a quadrant of the fourth and fifth dimensions in the astral plane. They had refused to give up their physical existence, so they remained hovering in exile, feeding off those that were still in body. They tried to feed off your energy that night. They were like gnats around a ripe piece of fruit with small voices. They mocked you, they called you foul names, and kept disrupting our evening lesson. I was very angry at you for allowing that man to touch your hand. But you were innocent of the darkness. You did not even know of its existence, for I had shielded you from that. So I and the other guides removed those leeches from your soul, as you slept that night, bringing them forcibly into the light, to rid them from your being. That is something we do not usually do. Then we began teaching you how to protect yourself with the light, so you would be a victim no longer."

"I remember," she said gravely.

"It was your first lesson of their existence. You have had another since then, which was much more serious. Your cowboy is unaware of these elements. Because of his darker nature, these beings are attracted to him as they were to that man at the bookstore. Because of his alcoholism, he is vulnerable to their attack and possession. When he is drunk, he has no defenses to prevent them from taking control of him. He will be completely helpless to stop them. He will hear their voices as his own. There are stronger entities than what you felt that night, entities which have fed for centuries off of mankind's negativity, fear and darker side, and have grown quite powerful in their progress. They are commonly known as demons."

"Because of your work with the light, you draw their interest. Truly they wish they could be like you, but they are unwilling to do the work necessary in their own growth. So, in anger and in jealousy, they wish to destroy what they covet, for they are denied it. The dark sides of their natures have grown to the point of shrouding their light sides. They cannot be of the light until they ask for it, and with the asking must come the acceptance of Christ, who would forgive and heal their beings in the appropriate way. But, they do not want to be healed, so they will remain in this dismal state until they are ready for love and forgiveness. They despise Him and all who represent Him. They wish to keep mankind in fear and in darkness, so they will not be alone, for that is the way they are in their souls."

"As Christ would heal and enlighten the world with his love, so would his brother Lucifer, who is also a child of God, darken the world to his description, breeding fear and destruction throughout mankind. The dark forces want to keep the living world as their feeding ground. They have infected the minds of mankind since the beginning of time in a constant struggle for superiority. You know it as the battle of good against evil. This war is beginning to escalate towards a final resolution in the twenty first century, when all mankind will join together in a more enlightened fifth dimensonal reality. All of mankind, whether wittingly or unwittingly, will play a part in this."

"I don't understand Matheu. Where does evil come from? Who are demons and how do we fight them so the battle can be won? Are we all not a part of each other and God, even them?" she asked.

"All things, including evil, come from God. There are those souls who have chosen to grow within the light, and there are those souls who have chosen the darker path. The gift of free will has allowed this since the beginning. Ultimately, you can not fight them. It is not your place, nor the place of any other soul to conquer them. You are not God, nor am I. This battle is reserved for Christ himself, for only he can heal them, and bring them back into the light where they belong. It is your job, and that of the individual soul to focus on themselves, making themselves whole. That is the best way to win, for it denies them their existence."

"You see, by challenging them in fear and in anger, you infuse them, giving them strength and validating their beings. They rise to the challenge. That is what they want, to divide the world into hatred, bigotry and anger, into countless conflicts of personalities, homicides and even genocides, instead of uniting all under God through Christ in peace and love. The world is their smorgasbord and they are like psychic vampires feeding from the weaknesses and prejudices of mankind. All are involved, whether they want to be or not. Ignorance of their existence is no protection. Does God not exist outside of belief? So do they, for you do not have to believe in something for it to be happening to you."

"Now, they do not feed off ordinary anger. I am not talking about the kind of anger one feels at a justifiable moment. I am talking about the anger that comes from vengeance and that calls for blood. When you are angry at your child for misbehaving, that is different. That anger comes from love and justice. When you are angry at a social injustice, that is different. That comes from wanting to better the world. When you are angry at a waiter for dropping soup on your lap, that is also different. It knows a beginning and an end and it teaches a clumsy waiter to be more careful. But when you are angry from the heart of your soul like a vicious animal seeking to attack, when your mind is filled with the poison of hatred and destruction, when you despise all or a portion of mankind for any reason, that is the kind of venomous anger I am referring to. Many people hide their dark sides behind the illusion of a common cause. Hitler did so, for he pretended to hate the Hebrews, when truly, he was consumed by his own darkness, and he hated himself."

"Even those that may appear to be righteous are their tools in this world. Those leaders that speak of the division of races are creating the division. Those that wish to dominate for whatever the cause are being dominated themselves. Those that malign or ridicule, *be* it one person or an entire civilization are nothing but puppets in the hands of the dark master. All are one, for God sees no division, but simply his children, whom are all loved equally and unconditionally in his heart. In division, there is victory for them and a world of fear, darkness and despair. In unity, there is God and a world of unlimited love, peace and prosperity."

"When confronted by them, as you have been, and will be again, do not be afraid. Call upon Christ and turn the battle over to him. He will not fail you, nor any other who calls upon Him. He is your greatest warrior, and by calling Him, you will be undefeatable."

"You see, my dearest Astarte, we are all soldiers of the soul, whether we recognize it or not. In truth, true evil does not exist beyond ourselves, but is a part of us, balancing out our beings, and allowing us the free will which serves us in our growth. Within each individual soul is both the dark and the light in perfect symmetry. For each of us, it is a constant battle to keep this precarious balance. When one side becomes larger than the other, that is our choice, and becomes our ultimate destiny. They are like us, but they are consumed by their dark side, as we are consumed with our light side and the goodness of our nature. As we represent the Christ within, so do they in their darkness

70

represent Lucifer and all that comes with him. They are the antithesis of the light."

"For mankind, this precarious balance of good and evil does not end with our death, but continues with us in our progress, as we rise like pilgrim's headed towards a spiritual mecca of perfection. Mortals are nothing more than spirit in body, and when physical death occurs, the individual soul transcends death, by leaving the body behind to this planet from where it comes, to continue their path into the higher dimensions of existence as soul beings."

"If you think God's hand did not create the essence of evil, which is intermingled in a symbiotic realtionship with the essence of good, you are sadly mistaken. God's energy is in everything and all are a part of Him and ourselves. Every action is his action, as we are all tributaries of this greater river of love called God. How we choose to flow is up to us, and sometimes our beings boil and bubble and sometimes they flow quite gently downstream, leading us quietly and peacefully to that greater ocean. It does not matter, for we are all going to get there sooner or later, the darker or the lighter, through a self created Heaven or Hell to acknowledge the source."

"We fight that part of ourselves, which manifests itself in fears, deceptions, and that uncontrollable anger towards others. We are free to choose how we grow and because of this we are in constant battle with ourselves, good versus evil, and sometimes the good wins, and sometimes the bad wins, but ultimately we never lose, for we are all learning as we go and have infinite chances to redeem ourselves, as we are all eternal beings and part of the whole."

"You see little one, we are all one being. We are all interconnected through God to form an immense network of life, and there is a constant interchange of elements and energy between us at all times. What happens to one of us affects us all, and the echo of our actions can be felt throughout the universe. Imaging a pebble thrown into a lake, causing a ripple that is felt within the entire body of water. Such is the current of life. One man's deeds are not his alone, but part of the collective whole of humanity. One humanitarian, one good man, can affect a positive change on the entire network of life, for the rest of the world, or even the universe. One man's negativity can darken the network of life, or the whole. This includes those in other dimensions and in other planetary systems, which are limitless. Humanity is not alone. It just feels alone, for it has created barriers which deny and distract from that connection which maintains its very existence. These barriers which mankind has created are in his mind. They are an illusion of man's thoughts and fears. This connection, the network of life, still exists whether we are aware of it or not. One must only turn on the light inside to see it, feel it, and finally, acknowledge the splendor of it all, instead of sitting depairingly in the dark, feeling alone. Even those that are consumed by their dark sides, are a part of that network of life."

"In the network of life every action counts for each contributes to the greater whole of the the world we live in. Sometimes the world is a darker place when the negative side takes over for the majority, sometimes the world is a lighter place when more of the positive side takes over."

"When the dark side takes over, the dark entities get stronger, and negative things happen to individuals and to society as a whole. There are misunderstandings, murders, and even wars, which wipe out entire populations. One person's negativity can spread like a cancer. When the light side takes over, good things happen, such as understanding, love, tolerance and unity. Then there is no fear. One must decide daily if he wants to be a a part of the darkness, or a part of light, for one affects the entire balance of the whole and is responsible for all."

"This darkening process is called the cycle of negativity, for negativity spreads quickly as a flash fire does, consuming all in its path, until the release is over and it burns itself out. Then the positive side restores the world into its proper balance. Universal law demands this balance, and one side cannot exist without the other. Neither side is abolished but must all blend, ultimately, into harmony with the other, rising to perfection, no matter how long it takes. The path is freely given, and each individual must decide for themselves. But never doubt that all come from God, and all go to God, and there is no judgement on anyone, only actions that are either positive or negative, in one way or another."

"We see God in everyone, though we know some actions are hideous, while some are miraculous. All will be dealt with and answered for over time. Balance will be achieved, justice righted, and everything will come out all right in God's hands and in God's time, though it may not seem so when you are lost in the moment, drowning in the current of everyday life and it's events."

"As Christ represents all that is good, Lucifer is the Antichrist who represents all that is evil. His presence is necessary to give man a choice in his growth through the gift of free will, and also to balance the light. The light would not be so bright were it not for the contrast of the dark."

"Just as Christ has his followers, so does this prince of darkness. There is a breed of mankind that has not risen in death into the levels of transformation and the healing light. They have died, but have remained stuck in their stubborness and in their pain. Instead of asking for help from their guides, they remain in their diseased souls in the lower levels of the astral planes. They are the mass of his army. They are formless, and full of fear and anger, for they wish to be alive, committing foul deeds as they used to while they were enjoying the flesh. They stubbornly refuse to love or to be loved. They are not alive in the physical sense, but refuse to accept their spiritual existence. They are in a no man's land, a void without beginning or end, until they acknowledge God and ask for his forgiveness. They are just above the heads of vulnerable mankind, and are looking for ways to interfere in mankind's choices and his growth. Ultimately, they wish to possess mankind, and restore themselves to full existence. The astral plane of nonexistence, which is neither physical, nor fully spirit, is hell to them. They invent games to amuse themselves while feeding off of mankind's fear. Fear gives them power and strength. Love and harmony drives them away into a place where they do not want to go, which is the beginning levels of the healing light, where they will be forced to face themselves, and where help and healing is awaiting them.

All they must do is ask for this redemption, and the process will begin."

"They are masters of communication to ordinary mortals that are weakened by negativity, such as people who are emotionally wounded, alcoholics, and drug addicts. To the positive and the strong, they are nothing but annoyances that plague you at times, and are hardly noticeable. They are weaker than us, and their only weapon is their projection of fear."

"They are quite capable of placing themselves into the souls of some animals, who will frighten or attack you, or into humans who have been weakened over time through intense pain, fear or some outside stimulus. Fear is mankind's greatest enemy, for fear attracts them like sharks to a feeding frenzy. They create more havoc in the world than they are given credit for."

"They inflame hatred in any way they can. There are many groups that support and feed them, housing them in their negative energy, either knowingly or unknowingly. These entities do not hate one group or another, but hate all humanity, only disguising their feelings in the illusion of racism and religious differences. They are jealous of those in body, for they want the same freedom and experience that they have lost. They fear those in spirit, for they cannot have the blessings or the strength that they have not earned."

"There is a hierarchy in the universe based upon the growth of the soul within the light. In balance, there is a hierarchy of darkness. There are dark forces that are stronger than the lower elements that we have spoken of today. They are comparable, shall we say, to the archangels, though not quite as strong. Because of your work as a channel, these stronger forces have become interested in you. Do not be afraid, for you are fully protected by your soul, and by your companion angels, of which I am but one of many. Let us just say that your soul is a tough old soul and has dealt with them many times before. They do not like her for she has beaten them. I, myself, am not even your strongest protector, though you in your love for me, may believe it to be so. I would like to be."

"But these darker entities have found a new avenue to reach you. Your cowboy has a much darker energy than yours, and is vulnerable to them through his pain and his drinking. Because of this, he is not protected as you are. He is open to them and will remain so, because he chooses it, and also, because it is his path at this time, to conquer them on his own. He is not as strong as you are, though it may appear to be different in this reality with his masculinity and his bravado."

"Little one, this is not an illusion, but the reality of true evil. No incarnation is a match for what we speak of. In innocence, you will find much strength, for your soul and other elements of the light will naturally protect you. Do not directly invoke them, for in a physical showdown, you would be destroyed. Trust in God and allow Him to shield you. In the physical world, can you stop a bullet and survive? Can you stop a animal from attacking you? Your children are at risk, or will soon be, when you merge into a family. Remember the cowboy and what he risks in himself, for he has no knowledge of this. He drinks to ease his pain, and nothing more. He is their victim, and unknowingly, part of a larger plan. But he unwittingly plays into their hands. When you are speaking to him and he is in control of himself, you will know. When his drinking escalates and he is not in control of himself, but has been invaded by a darker energy, you will know that too. It can happen in a second. When it does, walk away. He will not remember those times, because it is not completely him. You cannot save him. Only he can save himself through his own faith, which lies between him and his God. That is his healing."

"The war between these forces will result in the rebirth of Christ, not only in physical form, but through the unified hearts of mankind, to lead humanity to unconditional love. There will come a time, when there will be Heaven on Earth, as there was at the beginning."

"These dark elements will try to prevent that in any way they can. At that time they will lose their feeding ground and their stronghold. This will have a universal effect on all the dimensions, for they will be forced to progress into the light, to begin their healing process. They will have no where else to go."

"Many souls are involved in preparation for this, and they will all be targeted in lesser or greater ways. I have told you that

75

the work you do, you do for everyone, that the world may know of God's unconditional love. They would stop you if they could, for you cannot see where your purpose may lead. A person's work extends beyond him, touching the lives of many others. Even your actions can affect the network of life."

"This will not be finished in your lifetime, for it is only the beginning of the change. During the lifetime of your children it will escalate, and they too, will serve in their own way. It will be completed during the era of your grandchildren. But that is all you need to know, that your lineage will stay true to your faith and carry out your legacy over time."

"You see Astarte, in the twenty first century, humanity will discover that they are not alone in the universe. Many already know this, but proof will be given, and the light will be turned on for those remaining in the darkness. The galaxies and other dimensions will open up to the world, and mankind is being prepared for these revelations. But mankind must first accept his fellow man in the network of life with unconditional love, before he can accept any other beings that may bear different forms. Mankind upon awakening must make their own choice between the darkness and the light."

"Much will be revealed to humanity in the coming times as they grow nearer to this. They will begin to understand the creation of life itself. The power of creation is a great gift, but with it comes an even greater responsibility, for it is more than a science. One must learn to value all life, even if it is different from their own. One must then learn to use that knowledge of creation for the good of all."

"It saddens me to say that much of humanity is intolerant of each other. Man is constantly judging his fellow man through race, creed and religion, and other petty social means. Much of mankind chooses to highlight the differences, instead of the similarities, and the common bond shared between them. All are an equal part of the network of life, and together create one great universal being, united under God."

"Mankind is being prepared for the time when this bond will be recognized. Until humanity acknowledges the brotherhood of all, his eyes have been intentionally shielded from the discovery

76

of other beings in other galaxies far away and also, in other dimensions of time. Time travel will become possible as mankind is given this gift of vision, for as you already know, all time is one. Now, only those that have achieved a clarity of heart and oneness of spirit have earned the right to this vision. You are one of a minority that has been allowed access to this information and experience. The majority of the population only entertain these possibilities for their own amusement, they do not believe in them."

"A higher energy is coming to this planet which will be obvious even to the oblivious. The earth itself will slowly move on its axis by degrees, which will put this planet and its inhabitants directly into the light. The earth has always been in the light, of course, but never directly in the light. It has always been in refracted light, to allow humanity more time to slowly grow to awareness."

"You are accustomed to the light because you work within it every day. Yet, even you will feel the change. To those who have never experienced it's intensity, it will be a shock to them. Your work within the light has made you stronger and opened your psychic vision to the various dimensions that lay before you. You are ahead of the game. For those who have lived in negativity, fear and inner darkness, the light at first will blind them, for they will feel immobilized and paralyzed by the pressure from within. Not only will there be external changes in the world as you know it, but there will be internal ones in its people. This will ultimately raise the energy and vibration of those living on this planet, with a clarity of vision that they have never experienced before."

"It will alter the environment and the perceptions people live by. It will eventually bring unity, and a time of great peace and love through its healing energy. But first, it will bring uncomfortable feelings as everything intensifies individually and as a whole, until the transformation is complete."

"Some will ask you, what is the light. You may tell them that the light is an energy, or a current that runs through every living thing in the universe, connecting all to its source, which they know as God. It is the blood of his being. It is what brings life

77

and animation to the network of life. It sustains our souls as well as our bodies and it is the healing light of God. In religious terms, for those who prefer, it can be called the Holy Spirit, only it is without personality. It is a force. It cannot be decribed in words, for it is unlike the sunlight, or the moonlight. Those lights, however beautious, are weak in comparison. But like them, it can be felt in its intensity, and it can be called upon and directed to perform what one would call miracles. The light, itself, is the miracle of all life."

"But, it is very strong, and within its presence things rapidly change. You see, in the dimness, people repeat the same lessons over and over again. Within the light, life becomes increasingly clear and vibrant, and people are forced to complete their lessons at an accelerated rate of growth. Just as a plant grows stronger and faster in the sunlight, so do people grow stronger and faster within this intensified light."

"To grow, people must face hard lessons, so sometimes what the light may bring is not what would have been chosen to be learned by the individual personality. I speak of the soul lessons the individual is born to complete, that the individual personality may wish to delay. Who will wish to face lessons in greed through loss of money or love through bad relationships? There are an infinite amount of lessons as there are souls. On the other hand, there are many rewards coming for those souls who have completed their individual lessons."

"But because of this, it will be a slow process to avoid disaster. Through this change there will be some turmoil, as nature reacts to the gradually growing light, with storms, earthquakes, and tidal waves. There will be an overall global warming resulting in some flooding. People, unused to this greater energy, will feel their emotions much more strongly, either positively or negatively, and they may tend to overreact, in love or in anger, depending upon their emotional climate during this transition. There will be much more violence within the population. Children will be especially vulnerable as they are more open than adults."

"Eventually there will be a polarization of thoughts and emotions. By this I mean there will be a separation of the positive and the negative elements within the population. Those who have positive energies will become more comfortable within the direct light and begin to flourish, spreading their joy to others, while those who have darker natures and who have lived their negativity, will find the climate intolerable. They will act out their aggressions, until they slowly wither and die through natural or unnatural causes. People will become more of what they truly are. There will be a cleansing within the population. Those that are too heavily damaged will return to their soul forms, where they will proceed with their growth and their healing in another dimension at a much slower pace. Some souls will voluntarily leave, to assist with the healing in other dimensions. With help and love, all will be properly attended to. No one will be forgotten, abandoned or lost."

"Those that survive and remain here, will be allowed to continue into the new century with their lives, contributing to mankind's evolution and expanded positive growth. The earth, within the direct light, will become part of the greater collective of the universe, and man himself will become multidimensional as he was meant to be at this time."

"As Christopher Columbus brought the world into the third dimension, so will the light now bring this era into the fifth dimension. The third dimension already existed during Columbus's time, though it had never been seen by the human eye. Columbus was a visionary. The fifth dimension also already exists, though it too has only been seen by visionaries, many of whom are channels."

"The next years will bring about many changes which you will be a part of. You, and many others like you, will teach the rest of the world about what is happening, calming their fears and bringing them more easily into the light through your own well established faith. You and your comrades will silence the doomsdayers and the religious phanatics who are predicting the end of the world. There will be an increase in suicides as fear grows during this volatile period. Many individuals and religious groups will begin to hoard food and to behave erratically desperately trying to protect themselves from what they fear is the end of the world, but the only true protection lies within.

They spread false fear for they have not developed true faith and cannot see past their own darkness. It is not the end, but the beginning of a new era."

"You have been taught the healing arts by spirit throughout your life. But the most powerful form of healing is through the essence of yourself. It is through your presence, and through others like you, that many will heal, for they will believe in you as your cowboy does, and your energy will assist them through their transformation into faith. Your fire will ignite the fire of many hearts around you. But this will come much later when you least expect it. It is part of the natural order of things. Remember, true healers need nothing but their energy."

"None can escape the changes that are about to come, for it will affect the entire network of life. But fear not, for fear is mankind's greatest enemy, holding them back and destroying their vision and clarity of heart. This is not Armageddon, for that is a day of judgement. This is the Resurrection, with the continued opportunity for growth and love by a universal God who loves all beyond measure and whose Son returns to bring that love into final being."

"This is your destiny and how I raised you to be. There will be times in the future when your despair will challenge your faith and when you are most afraid, I want you to remember that God, is a constant provider and protector, who nourishes and supports us. Mankind looks for God on the outside, wondering whether he even exists. Yet, proof positive lies within, for the miracle of his love is self evident in all of our hearts, where he has always been a constant source of unconditional love to us, even though there are those who do not acknowledge his presence."

"You will accomplish many things in your lifetime. But your deeds are not your deeds alone. They are connected with all universally, for better or for worse, and they all come from Him directly, for you are a living part of Him."

"He hopes that each and every one of his children will care for the other, as He cares for them. This would turn the network of life into a positive flow in which all could prosper, united and healed. To love unconditionally is the highest form of love. It is without reservation, restriction or judgement. This is how you must love your cowboy. Remember you are your father's daughter."

"It is your choice. If your heart is filled with fear, then your outer world will be fear filled and full of failure. If your heart is filled with joy, then your outer world will be filled with joy and the success that it will bring. It is that simple. All life is a mirror of self."

"Through fear many painful illusions are created, such as the illusion of abandonment. These illusions are barriers which block the flow of life. We must remember that through our vital connection to God, we are never alone. How can one be abandoned, if one is part of the network of life? We are all interconnected. We must go quietly within to feel that connection and to utilize that support. Through this knowledge fear of abandonment becomes abolished."

"Mankind's greatest fear is that of death, and the ultimate separation from those that they love. But there is no death, just a physical transformation back to one's original form of spirit. One soul may still communicate and bond with another soul even after physical death, as you well know."

"Fear is the ultimate weapon of the dark forces, for it creates a spiral downward, which destroys all things in its wake. Faith allows love and life to bloom. Fear is a dangerous illusion that destroys that power of faith and blocks the essential flow of life that will resolve all conflict."

"There will be times when the fear of losing each other through the power of darkness will seem great. Know that your love which makes you vulnerable, will also keep you safe."

"At your greatest moment of fear, remember what I have taught you. The flow of God is like a great river. Sometimes the water is turbulent, sometimes it is smooth, but it is always unfailing in that it will carry you beyond your fears, if you will let it. Go with its essence, do not try to control or to change it. Become of it. That is the essence of spiritual growth. It will make you stronger, for you will become one with the God force, and that will see you through, no matter what happens, providing all that you will ever need. If you will allow it, the flow will carry you beyond the hurt into the healing. That force which gave you each other, will heal you both when the time is right, and you are both ready for that healing. In God's time and in the time of your souls."

"Remember that we are all cloaked in different disguises. You are currently cloaked in that lovely physical form. I am currently cloaked as a guide. When we remove these outer cloaks, all that is left is our energy, which is a reflection of our inner self. It is like the fable, The Emperor's New Clothes. Our disguises are nothing but an illusion of our true selves. Some energies are brighter than others, some are darker than others. It is dependent upon our choices and on our growth, and how far we have come to reaching that perfect reflection of brightness which resembles the energy of our Father and His Son."

"But for some it is much more difficult. They have many layers of darkness to strip away that have accumulated since birth. The constant layering of one painful experience after another, has led to the growth of their darkness. Such is the fate of your cowboy and many others like him."

"You know in your heart that the voice of fear and anger which you hear from him is not his true voice, but the distorted voice of his pain covering him. You can clearly hear the voice of his true heart, which is struggling to be heard above the din."

"You see, he has no memory of the light. His childhood was too catastrophic. Within the light all becomes very clear. One's feelings, one's purpose, and one's path, all blend into a knowingness within the light. There are no questions there, only answers. The interconnection between all becomes plain to see as well as the connection to God himself. All fear and all anger, which are merely distortions of the truth, melt away into faith."

"Within the light there is a cleansing of the bitterest of tears and a healing of all wounds, layer by layer, until there is nothing left but the true self. Like peeling an onion, one is slowly stripped, as all layers of doubt, sadness, fear and anger fall away, leaving only the soul self of beauty, peace and grace. Only what is real lasts within the light. If you lose something, do not mourn its passing, for only what is truly yours will remain with you forever within God's light."

"There are many levels of light. As one progresses within these levels, one becomes more whole. This can begin within the physical existence, or much more intensely, after the physical body has been shed. It is a constant process of the shedding of all illusions, resulting in the true self. You have basked within the light for many years, through my exercises and instructions, purposely and knowingly. At least I knew that was the way."

"Your cowboy has not, but has remained shrouded in the darkness of his pain and fear, adding to the many layers already covering him. This has stunted his growth. You are his introduction to that light. But it will take a very long time for all of his layers to be peeled off."

"Mankind was not meant to become so disconnected from the light. The third dimensional reality of man's world is filled with the illusion of struggle and strife, and mankind has felt abandoned by it's Creator. With this feeling of abandonment, humanity has drawn further away from the universal truth and the knowingness that it will be taken care of. It has drawn away from the light. This has made it vulnerable to attack from the darker forces. This illusion of fear is withholding mankind from his rightful place in the universe. With these coming changes, these layers will be stripped away over time, until the truth and the light emerge as the core of humanity."

"Through the eyes of fear, the world becomes a vista of nightmare illusions, so real that all clarity of vision is lost. Looking through the light one can clearly see the truth, and nothing is insurmountable. Within the light, there is no fear, and one is protected as you have been. I am not talking about minor fears. I am talking about fears so great that they take on a voice of their own, to the extent of possessing one's own body, mind and soul, as they have done with the cowboy over his lifetime of accumulation of these great fears."

"That is the voice of the dark side of the personality, which echos through the soul to the darker forces. Within the light there is complete safety, and a different voice to be heard. That is the frequency of the light that resonates with the angels. But when the darkness becomes so great as to eclipse the light, and fears take hold of the personality to eclipse all faith, when one's defenses become lowered and one's perspective distorted, one becomes vulnerable to the predators of the darkness which would do one harm. In combination with drugs or alcohol, it becomes even more deadly, for possession can take place."

"This happens all the time in the physical reality, though most people are unaware of it. Fear manifests more fear, problems and negative events. When bad things happen, people do not understand the combination of elements that make them occur. They will question God's will and his love, when really it has been a combination of bad choices made by men themselves that have opened the door to these tragedies. God's gift to mankind is free will to create his own destiny."

"Without this knowledge they are merely victims. With this knowledge they become co-creators of a better reality, and a better world. They are not powerless. They can assist in righting the balance through their own lives, to lead the world to a state of grace. It is their own choice."

"There have been men in this world who have committed foul deeds in their lifetimes. The world asks itself, how can this be? How can God allow it? I tell you, it is not allowed by God, but has been chosen by man, and has been encouraged by the climate of his environment."

"Some of these men have openly admitted to hearing voices, directing them to slaughter. These voices come from the dark sides of their souls, which are very large, and have attracted those pariahs who eagerly wait for an opportunity to create harm on the living, from their self created hell in the darker dimensions. You know who these voices are, even if others do not."

"Your cowboy has a great thirst for the light. As you progress down this path with him, he will draw upon your light and your strength unknowingly, and at times, you will feel drained of your natural resources and your energy. This will leave you more vulnerable to attack from those entities who would see you harmed. Stay true to your faith for in doing so, at your greatest moment of weakness, when all has been spent and all has been done, a greater protection will come. In your innocence, and in your truth, God will protect you both."

"Ultimately, mankind's perception of how he views the universe will change. Within the light, one will view his world with clarity and compassion. One will clearly see his fellow man and recognize the qualities within him. One will also clearly see spirit as they are meant to be seen. Few recognize spirit at all at this time. Many that do sense their presence see them indistinctly. Spirit are as man, individuals with traits and talents marking their individual beings, that exist at a higher vibration in the same time and space. If one views mankind from a judgmental and clinical perspective, one's vision will be cold and clouded, and both man and spirit will be distorted and dehumanized. Much of humanity dehumanizes itself and has also wrongly dehumanized God and spirit. Just as the essence of spirit is contained within mankind, so is the essence of mankind contained within spirit."

"The body of spirit resembles the physical body of man in form, though the substance is less dense. For man to understand the essence of spirit, he must first understand himself. To be spirit is to be the same as man, only in a different dimension. If one is stubborn in physical form, one will be a stubborn spirit. If one is disagreeable in physical form, one will be a disagreeable spirit. One is who one is and can only improve themselves through years of hard work and commitment. Remember, all time and space are one in the universe. All worlds are also one. One cannot become someone else, until one has mastered who one already is."

"You know this to be true, for you spend a great deal of time with spirit. You see spirit quite clearly and indentify them as individuals, with different appearances and personalities. Each and every voice is different to you. Each and every touch is different. Each guide has their own method of teaching and of sharing their experiences with you. You call them by name. Some, I might add, you like more than others. This is not an illusion, or a trick to fool you. What you see is determined by who you are. You do not dehumanize mankind, nor, do you dehumanize spirit. You see them as they were meant to be seen and truly are, in the same way you see your physical friends."

"All life is a continuous cycle of evolutionary growth. Life in the other dimensions is very similar to life in the physical third dimension, Spirit maintain their physical appearances, just as physical beings do for many reasons. They embody their physical appearance based upon that portion of their lives that best identifies their personalities. Some spirit may have lessons in vanity. Spirit, like man, is continually growing."

"I, Matheu, am your friend and mentor. Yet, there are others whom you may call upon, when you have something on your mind, in the same way you might call upon your physical friends. When you want a quick answer, you ask Adelaide, because she is sharp witted and to the point. When you want comfort and reassurance you go to Mary Claire. When you know that what you are doing seems impossible, you go to Damien, for he knows all and would refuse you nothing. Each one is different. The majority of mankind does not understand this. All they desire is the right answer, they do not care who delivers it, as long as it provides them with what they want. They do not acknowledge spirit for their trouble or even thank them for their continued assistance."

"You will meet those who will profess to know spirit, but they cannot decribe who or what they know. If you ask them who their guides are, they will say that it is a group conciousness. But I would ask them, who is in the group? Do they know them? I have always taught you to personalize your experiences and to identify who you are talking to, for all spirit are different from each other, just as all people are. Some are wiser than others. And not all are of the light."

"The universe is filled with individuals in spirit. Not all spirit are designated teachers. Do they know the skilled teachers from the unskilled ones? Should a channel identify its teachers as Jesus, Buddha and Gandhi, and offer their services for sale, would mankind believe they are who they say they are? I need not tell you that there is no charge for the love and guidance of Jesus and the other great ones. Their services are freely given to those who are ready for it. To be a channel, one must have soundness of heart, clarity of vision and good judgement to provide the best teachers and information to those who need it.

Some spirit are in process of growth themselves, and intrude where they are not supposed to be."

"How one relates to the physical world around them and to their fellow man is how they will relate to spirit and the greater universe. If they treat their fellow man with wisdom and respect, they will also treat spirit with wisdom and respect, and be assigned teachers proportionate with that level of growth. If they do not, one's teachers will be on the same level as they are and not very helpful. You will draw to you, a reflection of your inner self. A kindergarten student will not be assigned a high school teacher."

"It is easier to depersonalize something that you do not understand, rather than give meaning to it. I am part of the greater whole, as are all, but I have maintained my individuality throughout time, and will continue to do so. I was once a physical man, and I still am a member of that family of man, even though I do not have a physical body as you know it. But I do have a body, which you have seen and felt many times over."

"The physical world is nothing more than an entry way into the greater universe. It is preparation for what is coming. In that greater world of the universe, you will find the same things as you did before in the physical reality, only in a broader sense."

"Man creates his own reality in the physical world, as he does in the greater universe. Spirit builds their own environment in the higher dimensions, which is similar to the physical world, only they use their minds, for they are more in touch with themselves and their powers of creation. As they progress in their growth, it becomes, shall we say, a better environment, as the need for illusion becomes less."

"There is also a misconception in the human mind that spirit can be in several places at the same time. But that is with the telepathy of our souls, not with the true essence of ourselves. When *I am with you, all* of *me is with you.* Certainly, I am capable of answering your questions from afar, while I am in another dimension. But you are also capable of asking them of me in that other dimension, while you are sitting here reposed in the third dimension, simply by elevating your energy. That has nothing to do with our beings. Man and spirit are essentially doing the same thing in different dimensions."

"But we also have a personal and physical relationship. When I come to assist you, it is not a part of me that comes, but the whole entirety of me. I am not an overlay of energy, or a walk-in, or any other clinical term mankind has invented in its dehumanization of me. Nor do I send my left arm to enter your body while my right arm is doing something else. It is all of me coming to your aid with all that I am and all that I have to give."

"All souls are multidimensional, including those in body. A worldly psychic can sit in her chair in the present and read the future through expanding her energy. Yet, her energy remains intact, as does the energy of spirit. For spirit to visit someone, his whole essence must go. Where one piece of me goes, the other must follow naturally through its magnetism. That is the study of quantum physics. The ethereal body remains intact, as does the physical body which it resembles."

"Man does not allow himself to have a personal relationship with spirit. He prefers to keep them at a distance as he does with his fellow man. He does not wish to break the illusion for it would bring him too close to the truth about himself. He would see there are no easy answers. To become spirit will not change anything for him. For some it will make it even harder, for to be spirit means to be confronted with a greater intensity within the light. You can never escape yourself and what you need to learn to grow. Man cannot escape his humanity through death. He will be forced to confront it either in the physical body, or in the ethereal body. Man is much more comfortable with the illusion that he has created. Man perceives the world as a struggle and the after world as the ultimate solution. There is no instant wisdom or reward. The after world is nothing more than a continuation of what has already been on the physical plane. Individuals maintaining themselves and their growth through continuing lessons of hard work and ultimate achievement. Mankind is the father of spirit just as spirit has fathered man, and will still be, even in death."

"During this time, mankind's perception of God will also change. God is not limited, but mankind's perception of God has been reduced to the conflicting belief systems of a limited society. Mankind must look for God within the chapel of the heart, for He is always there and is available to all. They need not struggle to win God's love, for He loves all unconditionally, despite their shortcomings. But you see, that is how man feels about each other. They know not of unconditional love, but judgemental love."

"Mankind will see that there is no Heaven or Hell, only what they have created for themselves in their own evolution. But in their petty judgements and opposing belief systems, they damn each other. God does not. In the universe, one is never thrown away, lost, or forgotten, as in the world. All are welcome in God's temple, though in some religions, all are not welcome. They want you to earn what has already been freely given by God."

"The search for God is not new. The recent term for this search, the new age, is poppycock. What is occurring is nothing more than a continuation of the same quest which has existed since the beginning, for what was lost over time through mankind's own mistakes. There is no new age, only new illusions. Be it religion, phanaticism, or modern spirituality, it is all the same. From the Roman temples, to the cathedrals, to the hocus pocus psychic lines, it makes no difference. It is just more smoke, coming from the fire of the heart, where faith, unconditional love and God have always existed."

"Parents extinguish the fire in the hearts of their children without unconditional love. They have inherited this legacy of destruction from their own parents. That will change, for there will come a time when no one will ever be lost again, or the fire diminished within. All are born with faith until the world destroys it."

"There is but one age and one God, which has always been. God has never changed, but mankind keeps spinning the threads of its illusions, and will finally trap itself like a spider in its own web. Mankind need only go within themselves to find the truth. When they realize this, then all will be healed, and there will be no old age or new age, just a progression of mankind's search through different illusions to find the fire of the heart, and all time and purpose will become one in His unconditional love. God is finally coming home, if His children will let Him."

With that, they ended the discussion, and she went to sleep filled with the many things he had told her. The old guide watched her as she slept, marvelling at the strength of her faith and her love for the cowboy.

Her mind was set, and so was the cowboy's, that they would be together, come Heaven or Hell, he struggling with the darkness that threatened to invade his soul through his drinking, and she struggling to keep the candle lit for both of them.

Matheu stood by her bed in full physical form, gazing down at her as she lay sleeping. He thought of the young girl in armor in France a long time ago, and the price she had paid for her faith. He vowed it would be different this time.

The next morning she woke up eager to be with her children, whom she always missed when she was away. She thought of the cowboy immediately and felt safe knowing that he was a part of her life, even though he wasn't physically there. Matheu's words had not really sunk in, but had only brushed the surface of her mind.

There was no room inside her for words or for lessons. Her heart was full of love for the boy in Arizona, and full of faith that it would see them through anything that might happen. And though she had heard the words and the warnings within, she was not afraid, because to her, love was a force that superceded all obstacles and lessons. This was who she was, and how she had been raised by spirit.

So she spent her weeks away from him working with her guides and caring for her children. They spoke on the phone as much as they could. But even when she was busy, there was never a moment when she wasn't thinking of him. Because of her sensitivity, she could tune into him by allowing her energy to expand from the limited third dimension of her body into the greater reality of the fifth dimension, where there was no distance between them. There she could meet with the essence of his soul, touching his thoughts, feelings and observing some of his actions.

She was growing stronger in her ability to use her own soul to access information for herself, and when she had difficulty, Matheu was a very patient and dedicated teacher, who could tell her anything that she needed to know. She did these things in accordance with the laws of the universe, for as everyone knows, you cannot get information that you are not entitled to. The cowboy and his soul were open to her, as she was to him. Never would the guides or her own soul invade his privacy, for had this been the case, the door to his life would have been immediately barred.

She was happy with her children for she loved them as much as she loved him, but in a different way. Even though they were a part of her, she wanted them to grow beyond her into themselves. She was wise enough to know that her path and her expectations were not necessarily theirs, and they had the right to fulfill their own destinies. They did not belong to her anymore than she belonged to her own parents. God lends his children to earthly parents to raise, but then he expects them to be set free to create their own realities. So she nurtured them by giving them a foundation of love and faith in themselves and in the network of life, that they might grow up strong and free from fear. She was like a gardener caring for beloved flowers, nurturing them, but allowing them the freedom and the responsibility to grow into whatever shape and size they wanted to be independent of her. That was the only way she knew how to raise them, that they might fully blossom. To her, her children were the roses of her life.

But her feelings for him were different, for she knew that he would not grow beyond her into his own life, but into her through partnership.

Neither her love for the cowboy or for her children was greater, but complimented the other simply by its existence. There was no competition through loving them all, for as everyone knows, there is plenty of love in the universe, and the more one loves, the more one is able to love. And she could no more think of leaving him than she could them, for true love does not divide, but unites despite differences.

So they were all a part of her heart, and because of that, they were already a family despite the distance. When her children behaved badly she would gently rebuke them and it was the same for him. She could not abandon either based on behavior. She loved as one is meant to love, emulating the greater unconditional love of the universe. Through giving she received much more, for everyone knows that those who give unconditionally and without question always receive more than those that hoard of themselves and their spirit.

At times her inner world collided with her outer world, making her anxious about what was to come and wondering if she could handle it. When her anxiety got out of control, she knew she was out of balance with the greater force. So she would take time just for herself, to rebalance her own energy and to replenish her own spirit.

Sometimes she would take a bath as she had done in the beginning, soaking for hours in the light filled water of the tub, which soothed her. Or, she had another way that was less gentle and much more exhilarating. This time she felt that her older daughter was ready to join her.

Jodie was eleven, with a keen mind that perceived things way before they happened, and a loving spirit that was a pleasure to know. The angelic beauty of her face revealed the depths of her wonderful soul. Matheu had christened her Morning Sun, for her gently warming energy was all pervasive, yet tender, and reminded him of the sunrise which awakened the world each day in its glory. Now she was ready to experience more in terms of creating her own reality and spiritual growth, with her coming of age.

Jennifer, the youngest, was only six, and not yet ready for such a grand adventure. She was bright and peppery, with a deeper understanding than many adults and an infinite way of expressing that understanding. Matheu had christened her Fireball in her vibrancy. Still in her formative years, she was beautiful and spritely, as if the fairies had touched her, making her into pure loving sunshine. She was much more outgoing than her sister, yet, both shared a well of wisdom that was deeper than the ocean itself.

They were both beloved by spirit. To the girls, the guides were just a part of their family and each would go to them through their mother, with their own special questions and concerns, receiving information and answers with the gentle love and adoration of doting family members.

Both girls were beginning channels in their own right, though they were too young to understand it, and too busy with their childhood to be concerned about it. They just took that information for granted, like everyone glimpsed their future, and was raised by spirit. It was just a part of their everyday lives and who they were.

In their minds, they were no different than other children. Some of their friend's parents knew about other things that their mother did not know. Life had a wonderful balance.

Children are naturally connected to the universal force and if encouraged, they maintain that connection to become a permanent part of God and his greater faith. These children were taught to go within from an early age. Tragically, sometimes, this does not happen and some children grow up feeling disconnected from all things, isolated and abandoned by God, their parents and the rest of the world.

But this was not the case with these children, for they had many parents watching and loving them, both on the earth and off. Sometimes they might even feel that they had *too* many eyes watching them, for Matheu always knew what they were doing, and would catch them, before they could get away with something. Then he would laughingly and lovingly lecture them on the benefits of good behavior, saving them from a worse scolding from their mother.

The girls were always receiving vital messages from spirit in their dreams, and simply when playing, for everyone knows that spirit speaks to you at all times, and God is always there and a part of you.

So one night Fireball remained at home with her grandfather, to plot their own entertainment, while Morning Sun went out with her mother, Astarte, for a magical evening.

They drove quite a distance, until they found themselves farther out in the country and on a dirt road heading towards a grassy field. All around them the sky was open and clear, like pitch black velvet that had been strewn with a sprinkle of stars, glowing neon in the night.

There they joined a group of special friends, who had been tending a circle of fire all day long. They were the firewalkers, whose belief system was so strong, it allowed them to become one with the fire, so that they could walk, dance and play in it without getting burned. They were the masters of their own dominion, creators of their own reality and one with the God force.

The gigantic circle of hot coals was glowing in the center of the grassy field, as if a giant meteorite or pieces of both Heaven and Hell had fallen from the sky to ignite the world in a blaze. It was both fire and ice that night, as the coolness of the starry sky blended with the coals in the earth's grass, which were blazing hot at their feet.

Both mother and daughter could feel the heat rising on their faces and singeing their toes. The firewalk created an intense heat, where one could reach their full potential of energy by merging with the fire.

They would be living the prophetic words of Rudyard Kipling, "We be of one blood." The law of the jungle was also the law of the fire and the natural order of things. Man and fire would become one that night without harm. All things in the universe are one, and individuals could merge with the fire without being burned, simply by acknowledging that connection and by believing in it. But there was danger to those whose belief systems were not as strong or as developed as others. There was no room for error in this test of creating your own reality. Joy had done this many times before. It was her favorite activity. But for the child, it was the first time for her to test her beliefs by suspending all illusion from her being, to live the truth that she had been raised with and knew in her own heart.

They all joined hands and formed a giant circle of people around the huge fire. They raised their united voices in song declaring their faith. The singing itself raised their vibration and the intensity of their own energy. Pretty soon the energy of the circle of friends surrounding the fire became as intense as the circle of fire itself. The people began to glow with their faith and the fire of their hearts. They were ready, and one by one, as they felt the need, they walked out onto the glowing coals amidst the flames. Some danced in the fire, some sat down in it, some knelt in a prayerful position kissing the embers, giving thanks to their Creator for this great gift of confirmation in themselves and their own power.

The channel moved out onto the fire walking slowly, swaying to the sounds of the singing and feeling no discomfort. She felt as if she were walking on lumpy air instead of hot coals. She turned slowly in the center of the coals and stood there without moving, a central figure alone in the middle of the intense heat and glowing embers. Little tongues of flame lapped around her, like ocean waves breaking on the shore. She was mistress of the fire, becoming one with it, as she had with the greater force of the guides.

Her daughter stood mesmerized by the sight of her mother and stared with disbelief at the scene before her. She was frozen with fear. As a child she had roasted hot dogs and marshmallows over a barbecue pit, equally as hot, and had burned her fingers. Now, her own mother was standing in the middle of a giant barbecue pit, like a walking Oscar Meyer weiner, without getting burned. Then she remembered the truth in her heart. All you have to do is believe. Through faith, the impossible becomes possible very easily. You see, when she burned her fingers at the family barbecue it was because she was expecting to get burned. The adults at the barbecue had said, "Don't get too close to the fire or you will get burned." She had been prepared to be hurt. They had planted the seeds of a negative reality in her mind, and she had met their expectations by living that reality.

But these adults were very different. They were playing in the fire as if they belonged in it. They were not afraid. Her mother had been standing in the center of it for several minutes, and she had not been hurt. The child began to feel her courage growing within as she met her mother's eyes, and she began to move with it. The child's heart filled with the faith of her mother and of all living things, and everyone knows that faith and fear cannot exist in the same place at the same time. The faith in her heart so overwhelmed the fear that she made her choice to walk the fire without being burned.

Her mother stood in the middle of the coals, enveloped in the magic of the night. She held out her hand to her daughter to join her. Gingerly at first, Morning Sun began her journey into faith, each foot carefully placed one after the other, like walking a tightrope in the circus, slowly towards her mother waiting in the middle. She could feel the intense heat on her face, but it did not burn her, for her faith was strong to begin with and got stronger as she successfully conquered her fear. The more she walked, the stronger she got. Soon her timid footsteps were replaced by joyous ones, and she became a ballerina dancing with the fire. She reached the middle where her mother stood awaiting her. Faith always transcends disbelief. She joined hands with her mother and they started to dance together amidst the glowing embers, starlight on their hair, bodies glowing in the dark, as everyone sang and applauded the child's victory of becoming one with the universe and with her mother, who she loved and who loved her.

Their hearts burned that night with their love that was as hot as the fire that they walked, but their feet were cool and both returned home unharmed, filled with the faith of life, love for each other and the magic of the universe.

When they got home, they told the littlest one the story of their firewalk. Fireball told them that she had fallen asleep and dreamt of flying through the air with a wonderful magician in a long flowing robe, way up high where she had become one with the wind and the sky. The houses and the trees were very small, but she was not afraid for the man had held her very tightly. They had flown over a giant ring of fire, where she saw many people playing in it, as if in a field of stars. She knew that her mother and her sister were there. And he told her that one day she too would play in the stars with them, with fire in her heart. Then she had awoken to find them gently shaking her in bed. Both girls, that night, fell asleep in the greater arms of God, feeling safe, secure and strong, knowing their own power over their own lives.

This was their life together. They went to school, did their chores, want out to play as any typical family. But they always knew that their family was a microcosm of that greater family of the universe, including a God that loved them all unconditionally.

His life in Arizona was very different from their life in Pennsylvania. He loved riding with the wind on his face, the intense heat of the sun beating down on the broad brim of his hat, which shielded his eyes from the glare. As he rode, he felt the power of the horse beneath his legs moving with him and saw the mountains surrounding him, both challenging and rewarding him for meeting that challenge. He, too, was a microcosm of the universe and a part of the greater whole, though he was unaware of it.

He was a guide to those who trusted him to take them out into the wilderness. He vigilantly protected them and was like a wagon train master leading explorers and families alike home from their journey. He loved surviving in the rugged pioneer terrain without any modern impediments.

But lately something was missing, for he felt as if his life, which he had enjoyed, had lost its spark. He was slightly off balance and out of sorts with the people around him. It was as if the magic of the mountains was not as bright as it used to be.

His daily routine was becoming a struggle. At first, he thought it was the tourists and their constant chatter as he rode, destroying his thoughts and disrupting the peaceful panorama that lay before them. "If they would just shut up, I could enjoy the scenery and feel better," he muttered to himself. But even when they were quiet, he still felt restless and empty.

Then he thought, maybe it was his colleagues and his boss. "If they would stop pushing me so damn hard, then I would feel better," he muttered again in agony. But when he asked them to ease up, and they agreed, he still felt pressure from within.

Nothing seemed to help. It was then that he realized what was really bothering him. She was not there, but was back at home with her children in Pennsylvania. She was the magic in his life now and only her presence could bring him that peaceful feeling within. She valued him, and through her, he valued himself.

Then even though he loved the mountains and their beauty, he began to see flaws in them as he missed her. And though he enjoyed being with the tourists who adored him as their heroic figure, he became cross and short tempered with them, tired of their endless questions and their infantile needs.

And even though he had always gotten along with his fellow wranglers and his boss, he began to bicker with them, tired of taking their endless orders and shouldering his share of the routine work.

There was a time when he had wanted this job more than anything, but now he had found something that he wanted more. And he wanted it all the time. When he received praise from a guest that he had guided, he used to glow like a light bulb and feel enriched. He felt like he had been given a great gift, which was the gift of worthiness. But that seemed shallow now. The good feeling of the guest's praise soon wore off, but the feeling of being loved by her never seemed to leave him. He didn't have to earn it, like he had to earn the meager praise of the guests and their token tips. She just gave it to him. She loved him for himself and that was worth more than anything.

The need to be with her just seemed to grow inside of him, no matter where he was or what he was doing and nothing could satisfy the hunger within him when she was gone. She fed his soul, while others simply stroked his surface.

Even his boss patting him on the back, which used to make him proud, meant nothing compared to the gentle sound of her voice calling his name or the look in her eyes, which spoke legions of words in a silence so eloquent that it was beyond verbal understanding. It told him that she loved him more than anyone or anything in God's creation, Even more than he felt he deserved to be loved in his life.

He knew they were made for each other. She with her gentle nature and he with his stoic strength. It was as if they had been separated at birth, but had found each other again. Together, they were whole and had everything, while separate, they had nothing.

He wanted her there all the time and he did not want to share her with anyone, not even with her children. In his life people had cared for him and had even loved him, but it was always based on something. It didn't feel the same. Sometimes it was based on pity for an abandoned boy. Sometimes it was based on sex or his ability to party. Sometimes it was based upon the illusion of who they thought he was or who they thought he could be. Everybody thought they knew him, but nobody knew him like she did. He couldn't seem to get enough of her, so dry was the well of his soul. He knew something would have to be done to end these separations. But he didn't know what.

His logical mind told him that she had to go back to raise her children, but his heart was afraid of losing her. She always spent a week with him every month and the rest with her children, but it wasn't enough.

For years now, since arriving in Arizona, he had never left the security of the mountains to venture back into the civilized world. He had led a very secure and protected life there. All of his needs were met within the perimeter of the stable. He was afraid to go after her and to risk what little he had to join her in the larger world. He was afraid that the world would reject him as before. He was a caveman hiding in a corner of the twentieth century, and he didn't want to be part of the pretentious, civilized world. He wanted her to join him there in his cave, so it could be them against the rest of the world.

The world itself had forced him out by throwing him away. He had thought that he had everything he needed at the stable. He had a roof over his head, some money and plenty to eat. He had his horse, his saddle and his dog. When he needed friends, food, liquor or even physical comfort, it came to him. He had guided people from around the world, he was that good at his job. But they also came to him and he graciously or grudgingly showed them his mountains. They shared his world briefly and then they left to return to theirs. He didn't much care about them and they really didn't give a damn about him. He was a caricature to them of a mountain man and they were a caricature to him of what he was avoiding.

But with her it was different. *He* tried to force himself to put it out of his mind. "I'll think about it later," he whispered silently to himself, but her voice and her face surrounded him again and beckoned to him all the way from Pennsylvania, and something told him in his heart that he would give up everything just to be with her. Even his life if he had too.

He felt like he had been born to die his whole life. It was almost like he had a death seed planted inside of him growing since his birth. Drinking too much, living too hard, and always running away from everything. It was as if she had saved his life by loving him. Now, he wanted to live. For the first time he felt like he had a chance to be someone, if only he could overcome his pain and what he had been through in his past. But she didn't seem to care about what he was, or what he had done, or what he would become, for her feelings for him never changed based on anything. She saw the good within him, while the world did not.

He rarely drank when he was working. Oh sure, sometimes a wrangler would hide a flask of whiskey in his saddle bags and take a snort, or two, or three, while they were leading the guests. He was no different. But he took his job very seriously and the safety of the guests was his top priority. He was a professional. He would never put them at risk by incapacitating himself, so he always intensely controlled his desire to drink when he was on the job. But it was hard, for his real self needed to drink and he enjoyed the pain free relief that the alcohol brought him when the day was done.

So at night, taut as a drawn trigger, when the horses had been bedded down and the guests had gone, he would drink to ease the pain that had constantly haunted him since the day he was born.

Then sleep would come and he would dream of her, and what it would be like living in Pennsylvania as a real member of their family. To have a family of his own was always part of the dream. But sometimes, he would become jealous of sharing her affections and angry with the other family members for trying to take *her* away. Then he would wake up sweating and missing her. He wanted to learn to share her, but he didn't know how.

100

So he waited for the weeks to go by, when she would be returning to his side where she belonged, as if nothing had happened and the needs of the children had not come between them. Then he could feel the warmth of her love on his soul that was meant for him and no one else.

The world was filled with winter and each part was responding differently to it. In the east snow fell, nestling in the boughs of the green pines and the blue spruces, caressing both people and animals alike to a dream like hibernation with its winter lullaby.

In the west, the warmth and the intensity of the sun lit up the mountains, while the fresh, cool winter breeze sweetened the air from the tepid decay of the summer heat, blowing the sky clean of clouds and revitalizing the earth from the dry and dusty days of before, until all that was left were feelings of awakening and hope for a new beginning. It was from one to the other that she flew, from winter to winter, into the constant warmth of his welcome.

It was the snowbird season in Arizona and things were humming. He had been busy preparing for a big overnight camping trip at the same time she was preparing to come see him. This overnight was making him uncomfortable and he was dragging himself around trying to finish the packing.

He really didn't want to go because of her. She had been with him on many overnights before, with many different kinds of people, and they had always enjoyed them together, working hand in hand to care for the groups, like they were a team of horses pulling the same wagon. Always in step, they worked well together. She was a trooper and had adjusted to his way of life. She never complained, even when he knew she was tired, after riding all day long into the mountains, then setting up a camp to care for the guests. He had taught her everything that he could about his way of life. But this trip was different.

Part of him thought he ought to leave her in their room for just one night to spare her, but the larger part needed her there.

An insurance company had booked this trip as a gift for its female employees and he had been assigned as their guide.

They had already sent their gear on ahead, where a makeshift camp had been constructed to accomodate them. There were fifteen women going and included in their gear with the tents and the sleeping bags, the water and feed, was a ton of booze. This group had hard drinking on its mind.

He was not suprised, for this sometimes happened with large groups. The year before the same group had sponsored a similar event. The women executives that ruled with an iron hand, prim and proper in their facade, had let their hair down to become wild, drunken women on the mountain.

Looks can be really deceiving. He had learned that in his work. Sometimes the people that tried to impress him the most were the ones that let him down and impressed him the least. Those in authority that could have made a difference in the world, did nothing but think of themselves. They were like empty storefronts on a Hollywood movie set. They looked great on the outside, but inside there was nothing but maintaining their image for the rest of the world to buy into.

The world perpetuates its own myths about what is real and what is not, about what is important and what is not, by believing in the facade instead of seeing the truth.

These power women had shown their true colors on the mountain last year. Their facade had cracked and exploded, exposing the emptiness of who they truly were in his eyes. And they were no better than anyone else, though they pretended to be. Some were nice and tried to be helpful. But most were mean spirited, lewd and lazy sacks of shit, expecting to be waited on hand and foot. Some had gotten so drunk, they had run around half naked, fire water fueling them until they puked. Some even got so drunk sick they fell off their horses and couldn't ride safely back without help. Some seemed worse than his mother could ever be.

The possiblity of fifteen drunken women used to excite him. But now, he just felt afraid of her reaction to it. Last year, they had flirted with him, told dirty stories and generally made a fool of themselves. He had not touched them because they had no power over him.

102

She was so gentle, he was afraid to throw her into a situation that might make her angry, or change her opinion of who he was. He couldn't stop them from being themselves.

She was different from them. With her there was no facade. She never tried to impress anyone. She mainly kept silent about what she did or who she was. She was the same way on the mountain as she was off. She was a real lady and a class act. She could walk into a nice restaurant or get down on her knees in the dirt, washing the dishes in the horse buckets on a cold morning and be just as fine. He was very astute at sizing people up and he knew quality when he saw it.

But this was something he didn't want her to see about him. It was a part of his job to entertain them, they were paying customers and he did it well. But he did not want to be judged because of them. He wanted to be quality too. These thoughts played over and over again in his mind like a broken record as he gathered his equipment and waited for her homecoming later that night.

The flight was delayed from Philadelphia to Phoenix that day. She sat restlessly waiting in the airport surrounded by a blinding snowstorm that had pitted man against nature with neither side winning. After they were finally airborne, she felt her spirits rise. But nature was still fighting technology and the flight itelf became very rough. She began to feel afraid as the plane was jostled like a rambunctious child on the knees of the turbulent air currents.

Then she felt the energy of Matheu and heard his voice comforting her. He reminded her that angels guarded the plane from the callous wind, and that Haniel himself helped to protect the passengers. Haniel was an old friend. An angel of mercy, he healed the hearts of those wounded through love with his energy. He himself had intervened in the travels of many people bringing them to safety if he could.

She felt her fear waning and suddenly the ride smoothed out. In her heart she was already there. And whenever she feared flying again, she thought of angels holding up the wings and Haniel himself wearing the uniform of a pilot and she was filled with laughter.

The cowboy began to pace nervously. Sometimes her flights had been delayed, but this one was unusually late. He kept looking at his watch thinking something must be wrong. One am... Two am... He began to panic. He decided to call her house in Pennsylvania, not thinking of the time difference. A very sleepy child answered the phone.

"This is JJ in Arizona. I'm waiting for your mom and she is very late. Did something happen?" he asked the child without any further introduction or explanation. Of course the child in her wisdom already knew about him. She thought to herself, He must have it bad, but simply answered, "I'm sure everything is fine. She's on her way, but the flight probably was delayed because of the weather here. Goodnight." Then she sleepily stumbled back to bed, not worried at all, but wondering if he had a watch and could tell time.

So he waited pacing the floor, not realizing that he had just met a part of her that he feared. The night went on, but he couldn't sleep without the security of her presence and the knowledge that she would be safe and sound beside him again, where he could see and touch her, and most of all protect her, for he knew that she was very vulnerable out in the world without him.

She finally got to Phoenix at four am. The moon hung low over the mountains as she picked up a rental car and drove to the bunkhouse. When she arrived all the stable lights were on and he sat forlornly outside with his head in his hands on the stable steps. He rushed to greet her in a crushing hug that told her how scared he had been. They both went to bed that night realizing how difficult and dangerous the commuting had become for both of them.

The next morning brought the bustling activity of the overnight trip. He explained about the circumstances of the group and told her not to worry about it. He promised her that he would not drink. But he didn't ask her if she wanted to go with him. He just expected it. And she didn't question. Matheu had always taught her never to prejudge an event before it happened, because as everyone knows, it might turn out better than you think. They started organizing the remaining equipment, her helping him as best she could and staying out of his way when she couldn't.

After the horses had been saddled and everyone mounted, she sat astride her horse looking at the asssembled group. She saw fifteen women of various shapes and sizes. Some seemed friendly, some didn't, while others were openly flirtatious in their pursuit of the cowboys at the barn, like wolves in newly purchased women's western clothing.

She rode beside him as the long line of horses stretched out behind them. Just riding together calmed them both, and the parrot like chattering of their brood didn't seem to bother them, as they were followed like chicks trailing a hen to the henhouse. They rode hard until dusk to the campsite high in the mountains. It was a long ride but uneventful. He had his hands full though, constantly having to check to make sure that all the cinches remained tightened, and that no one fell off their horses.

There was much work to do in camp and no time to think about it. Seventeen tired horses had to be unsaddled, watered, fed and secured, while seventeen tired and hungry people had to be watered, fed and secured also. They did it together, with him caring for the animals and her cooking the chow for the guests. Working together made it easier and gave them the sense of unity they both had been seeking.

They were a good six hour ride from any form of civililization and as it grew darker she joked with some of the women and looked the other way as others openly flirted with him. The guests began their drinking, while he was building the evening campfire. She scraped steak for Sheba from the plates and then washed them in the horse trough in preparation for the morning's breakfast.

The women began to drink more and more, but he hadn't touched a drop. It was hard to say whether the bonfire or the fire in the women's drunken blood was hotter that night. It was as if he was seated in the center of flames that were growing warmer by the minute, as sexual innuendoes began to pass back and forth between the women, ignited by the sight of the only male within their reach. They were like vultures, attacking and pecking each other one minute, then preening and courting each other the next.

He sat watching her nervously, while trying to entertain them at the same time. He tried to comfort her with meaningful looks, not wanting to ignore the sacred boundaries of their love which stood out more firmly in his mind than ever before, but which were now being tested by these fifteen drunk insurance women seated around the campfire.

She thought of the firewalk and how easy it was to walk the hot coals. Somehow, this seemed harder and burned more. "Firewalks come in all shapes and sizes," she murmured to herself.

The women were pretty loaded when they began to pass a stick around to each other, taking turns with it to see who could tell the dirtiest story, when in the middle of the vulgarity, she got up and disappeared.

He looked for her in the group, but she was gone. He began to feel sick to his stomach, thinking that something was wrong and maybe she had left him. But he knew she couldn't go far in the middle of nowhere, on a mountain top in the pitch dark. "Maybe," he said to himself, "She went to the outhouse." He waited for a short time before finally realizing that she must have gone for a walk to get away from it all. He wished he could find her. But it was his responsibility to care for the guests. So he sat watching and waiting, but he couldn't see her in the surrounding blackness. Fear rose in him and he was silent amidst the noise and the perverse attention, feeling lost without love.

She began to walk farther and farther away from the cacophony of the camp and the hostility of the women, which was cloaked in their behavior of sexual innuendo. There was no refuge, for they were hours from anything. She was scared of the dark and lonely without his love. She was not angry at him, because she knew he was doing the best that he could under the circumstances. This was a part of his job and if she accepted him, she had to honor his work and take the bad with the good, whether she liked it or not. He was not drinking, though she knew he wanted to. He was doing it for her, and for the others who might get hurt if things got out of control. The guests were too far gone to fend for themselves and he was the only thing

106

that stood between them and the wilds of the mountain they had come to defile instead of honor.

She walked for awhile and found herself in a remote area. Going carefully around a bend, sidestepping cactus and rocks, she could no longer see the camp's light or hear a sound. Everwhere around her was pitch black and only gently illuminated by a slice of moon in the sky. She had to be careful because it was rattlesnake season and they were hard to see. She wished she had taken Sheba with her for protection. She knew he couldn't leave the group, and she wondered if he had even noticed that she was gone.

As she looked up, the sky was friendly and comforting, lit by many stars like candles on a birthday cake. She had never felt so abandoned as she did that night, with the man that she loved sitting around a campfire with fifteen drunk insurance women, while she was sitting alone in the dark with no way home. She was completely stuck and she began to panic. Sitting carefully on a flat topped rock, she prayed silently for help.

As she sat shivering in the darkness, which was both within her and without her, she knew there was only one thing to do.

She closed her eyes and she began to breathe deeply, until she was safely swimming in that sea of light that connects all levels to the safety of spirit. She called out inwardly with all of her strength asking her guides to protect her and to show her the way back from the wilderness of her fear. It may have been seconds or even minutes, she could not tell, for there is no time in that greater ocean. But when she opened her eyes, fully conscious and alert, she was still alone on the mountain, but something had drastically changed.

All around her, in full circumferance of where she sat, each and every living shrub, cactus, bush and tree, was lit by millions of tiny white lights. It looked as if countless fireflies had alit on every thorn, leaf and branch and were blinking a greeting to her. She felt an intense energy surrounding her, securing her presence in a circle of protection. She knew then that she was never alone, not even in the most extreme circumstances. The fear left her, as she wondered at what was happening, enchanted by the blinking lights.

She cautiously stood up and looked all around. Movement didn't change a thing. She was still completely surrounded by the blinking white lights. She looked up in amazement to make sure the stars were still there. They were and so were the lights around her, blinking on and off.

She had seen many wonderful things in her life, which were spirit themselves and displays of their energy. But never had she seen such a spectacle as those lights on the mountain that night.

She could see beyond the circle of lights into the further darkness of the desert and the mountain terrain. It was pitch black beyond their perimeter. She sat there for a long time, mesmerized by them, just watching and enjoying them, feeling very secure in their presence.

The mountains are filled with spirit who had come to her aid, because she honored them in her heart. Then, all of a sudden, she heard a voice. It seemed to surround her, coming from nowhere in particular, yet coming from everywhere. It said loudly and clearly. "To thine own self be true, for you cannot lose what is truly yours."

The voice had answered her question, for she had really been afraid of losing him to the drunken women. Love is not a competition, but a gift freely given, and everyone knows that it cannot be lost if it is true love and meant only for you. She sat there silently with tears in her eyes, thanking the mountain guides who had come to her rescue.

The lights stayed there with her, until she slowly got up and started to walk back to camp, going beyond the circle they had formed. As she moved beyond the circle, the lights slowly dimmed, then stopped, and the night grew dark again, as the mountain returned to normal. But she was no longer afraid. Gradually, the light of the campfire came back into view.

He had been worried and she knew it immediately by the way he looked at her. "Are you okay?" he asked. She nodded and smiled. He felt as if a great weight had been lifted from his heart when she sat down beside him.

In the midst of the continuing reverie, she said she was tired and was going to bed. Saying goodnight to everyone, she made her way to their tent, leaving him there with the others and laid down to rest on their sleeping bags.

She hadn't been gone but a minute or two, when he made his excuses despite many protests, checked on the horses, and crawled in beside her, taking her in his arms to sleep.

With the words of the mountain spirits ringing in her ears, she held him close and they fell asleep together, oblivious to the drunken illusion outside, safe in the truth of their own little world.

She knew then that you cannot lose what is truly yours, for it will survive the harshest of realities. So they were never without love from that moment on, even in the worst of times. And they were never alone for they had each other, and she knew in her heart that the arms of God and spirit were very long, for they had reached that mountaintop, but then, so were their arms for each other.

Their relationship grew against all odds. They had created a central reality in which they both existed and the rest of the world did not. They were two halves making a complete whole, individual, yet the same. Each of their personal realities seemed to lack what they had together. As time passed, the separations became more unbearable, and their souls pushed them harder for a complete integration.

"Soon he will be coming to Pennsylvania to live with you, little one. He is unaware of it now, but he will make the decision shortly. The separation has become intolerable for you both, and his feeling for you is far greater than for what he leaves behind. Don't question his decision. It is meant to be. Prepare a room, for he will need a space of his own to adjust in," Matheu said one day.

This was unexpected news. Pennsylvania was opulent compared to their lifestyle in Arizona. The east is filled with unnecessary excesses that the true west declines in its character. She knew that he felt safe in the mountains. It was hard to believe that he would give up his security for her.

She selected a bedroom in her house and decorated it with the western artifacts that she had collected in her travels. It was comfortably reminiscent of their bunkhouse room, a combination of them both and a western oasis in the eastern home of her family.

On her next trip they spoke casually about Pennsylvania. He seemed more interested than usual, probing into the smallest details of her life there. She described Meadowbrook and they laughed at the image of the fox hunters blowing their bugles in the wind, charging like a false calvary. She told him that he was always welcome there. He had a home in Pennsylvania too, she reminded him.

He had been growing edgier. He could not stand the distance anymore. He was fighting with his coworkers over trivial things, snapping at his boss, and pouting with the guests. He wanted to go home with her, but he was afraid.

In his mind he wondered how could he live in a strange and arrogant eastern world to care for a woman and two children that he didn't even know. He was just learning to give of himself. He had made all of the women that had come before her conform to his needs. But that was lust and came from a selfish place within his heart that he did not like to acknowledge even existed. With her, it was different. Now he knew the difference between lust and love. Love gives of itself, unconditionally and without doubt. He would do anything for her.

He quit his job that morning without warning. When she asked why, he simply said that it was because you need me and I need you and this is the only way to be together.

They packed up his belongings, rented a small truck, and began the long cross country drive back to Pennsylvania. They were a united threesome, her, him and the giant German Shepherd, who was a part of both their hearts.

He loved the beautiful horse ranch that was her home in Pennsylvania. He was taken with the children. He had never seen two little girls that were as lovely. To him, they were like miniature cameos of their mother.

He had left his own daughter behind long ago and hadn't seen her since, so they filled that giant gap in his heart as best they could. He refused to go back in his life to see her, so he forged ahead, and they accepted him unconditionally, because their hearts were open.

He enjoyed the foxhunters and their prissy eastern way of riding. They amused him with their formality and he would tease them by roping them with his lariat during rides. The stone mansion became his home, like the places he used to see on television and he reveled in the opulence. For the first time in his life, he felt that he had a heritage and was part of something. He finally had a family legacy and he loved the attention and the power that it brought to him. He was not a nobody anymore. But in his heart, he knew that he would have gone anywhere, as long as she was there.

He became the prodigal son, helping her father maintain the estate. In the evening he would ride the fences with his dog and rifle, guarding his home and his family. If anyone bothered her or the girls, he made sure it didn't happen again, and he became her fierce protector in the physical, as Matheu was in the higher dimensions. She was happier than she had ever been, for they were all finally together under one roof, the family that she had hoped they would be.

But she was very sensitive to his needs and at times she would sense that he was like a fish out of water, who could only withstand so much dry land. She saw that he needed the unrestricted freedom of the West for he began to drink more. She knew then that he had to go back. And as he had put her first and given up everything for her, she did the same for him.

By then her parents were ready for retirement, so she sold Meadowbrook, which was her legacy and a part of her heart, and she and the children prepared to move to Arizona with him for a new adventure.

"Little one, if you sell this property now, you will only get a small portion of what it is worth," Matheu said in warning. Then he told her the exact amount.

When the sale came, Matheu was right to the penny. But, her parents needed to move on for their own well being and they had to get on with their lives. She had never measured her family home in terms of money. It was a very valuable property. Yet it's true value came from the love that she felt for the land. It was painful giving it up. Still he meant more to her than anything earthly ever could, and neither's value could be measured in worldly terms. Her true home was in her heart with him and the children. She knew how much he had sacrificed for her in coming there. She was only doing the same for him. She had to get the cowboy home, and as everyone knows, money has no real value in the world compared with love.

The children were both in awe of him, for he was like a storybook character come to life. At times, he was very attentive to them, and at other times, he was totally withdrawn. He had trouble showing his emotions to anyone but her. But he tried, and would play raucously with them in that rough way that children play, having water fights all over the elegant household, and intense games of hide and seek, until all the furniture had been overturned and the draperies soaked, and she threatened banishment to each and every one of them. Then, in the next instant, he could become extremely authoritative, for that is the way he had been raised, and the only way that he knew how to raise them.

He became head of the family, but he had not yet learned the difference between power and love. At times he was harsh and controlling, and at other times understanding. Still, they stood by him, for their mother's sake, and also because they liked him.

During that time the forces of darkness fought over him, but in her home there was such a wealth of spiritual protection they gained no foothold. But she knew that they had to go, come what may. When the sale was completed, they left the sanctuary of Pennsylvania to move back to where they had started, the Superstition Mountains, as a family together.

Both of them loved Pennsylvania and all that came with it, but their hearts were in Arizona, and a simplier, independent life. She only gave up for him what he had given up for her and though the amount of money might have been different, the value, the sacrifice and the meaning, was exactly the same.

They bought a small ranch at the base of the mountains, and they were married there. For the first time, life was whole for them both. As the preacher married them, he clasped her hand so tightly in his and looked so deeply into her eyes, stating his oath of love to her, that she thought her heart would break. Her oath to him was no less felt, and for them both, their marriage came from the depth of their souls. She became the cowboy's wife, and he, the channel's husband in the eyes of the law, but it was always that way anyway, in the eyes of God and in their own hearts.

The more he loved, the more he drank for fear of losing that love. At night they would lie together and he would tell her how hard it was for him, fighting the demons of the drink which threatened to take him away. He was overpossessive of them at those times, because he was afraid they would leave him. As she lay in bed late at night, he would lie close to her and say that no matter what, he would always be there. Then, as she fell asleep in the safety of his arms, he would tell her a story, as if she were a little girl again. His favorite was "The Cowboy and the Princess". He would start it like this, "Once upon a time, there was a cowboy who roamed far away from home. But all he could think of, wherever he was, was the princess who was waiting for him to come back. And he always came back to her, no matter what." She would fall asleep with his words echoing in her ears. Her children were safe in bed, the world was complete within her heart and there was heaven on earth, because they were together.

Then, in the midst of heaven, the demon struck again. In a drunken rage, he grabbed a gun and threatened them. She and the children ran for their lives from the devil who possessed him. After that he went into voluntary rehabilitation to quit drinking, so ashamed was he at what had happened.

But the darkness had a foothold in his being and it wouldn't let go. And it was just as Matheu had warned, a bitter battle between the darkness and the light for his soul. Seeking professional help brought nothing, for he was unable to maintain his sobriety despite constant treatment.

The world condemned him, for they could not see his heart, only his actions, which were very different from who he was inside. Then they condemned her for staying with him. The modern world is a cruel place, for most people base their lives on shallow emotions and surface judgements, instead of on loyalty and unconditional love. Few understood, and saw the truth within them. Psychics only read the surface destruction. Only the channels could see the whole picture through their guides, and stood by them like pillars of strength in their higher vision, but the darkness was like a tornado taking everything else in its wake.

He would try to quit drinking, seeking the best of the worldly help available, but then would fall again, prey to the pressure of the darkness. There were times when, in the eye of the storm, he would be himself and then they were a family who had everything. At those times he would beg her to save herself and the children. He was afraid for them, because he could not control the drinking or remember his actions when that overcame him. He would never hurt them intentionally. But she knew in her heart where she belonged and would firmly stand by him and say, "No matter what happens I will never leave you. I love you more than anything." And he would gain strength from her love to fight again for his life. She saved his life with her unyielding love, for there were times when he did not love himself. She always restored his faith in himself, when the rest of the world did not believe in him. Then, he would again seek more counseling, for an enemy that came from beyond his reach, and beyond the power of the counseling to heal.

When she was alone, she would plead with the guides to heal him, tears streaming down her face, but it was beyond their power to do so. They would respond compassionately by telling her that he must choose to save himself by opening his heart to God. He was not open to their healing. And he always refused to pray. He could not forgive his mother for abandoning him, nor God for allowing it to happen. So the alcoholism destroyed everything, until all that was left was their love and faith in each other.

The children, though afraid at times, still seemed to thrive, and they grew up defenders of the light like their mother before them. They were both popular and excellent students in school, sound of mind, body and spirit. Unlike most, they had been raised with a high level of compassion, unconditional love and understanding. They had a stronger foundation than most mortal children, and as everyone knows, houses with a strong foundation can withstand any storm, while houses that only appear to be strong, collapse with the first gust of wind.

Other marriages came and went in time, built on the illusions of temporal love, but their marriage remained firm. Many who judged them lost their own relationships over time, or never found love at all, for as everyone knows, you cannot have real love if you do not know what it is.

One morning, after many years had passed when he been drinking constantly, bridged by rounds of rehabilitation to stop the drinking, Matheu said to her very gently, "It is too much to ask him to stop drinking. His physical addiction is too severe and it is beyond his mortal capabilities to stop. Either abandon him or accept him as he is. This is his destiny."

She knew that he was speaking the truth, for she had felt it in her heart many times before. Without hesitation, she chose to stay. She would go to Hell with him if she had to. She spoke with the children about Matheu's warning and they too, chose to stay with their mother and the cowboy.

At times the cowboy cried, for he had never known unconditional love, and could not reward it, for the alcohol firmly had him in its grasp and he was becoming the demon's puppet.

They lost their ranch, so they moved to a smaller home to make their last stand against the darkness. It took all of their money and most of their friends, as predicted, but it could not take the family itself.

The children explained to those well meaning people, who asked why they stayed together, "Would you leave someone if they had a disease, like cancer or aids? You would get them help until there was no more help available. But you would never abandon them, or stop loving them."

The periods of darkness were mixed with incredible periods of light, when he would show them the best of who he was, but the bottle would overpower him in an instant and he would become the demon again, losing control and the memory of everything that happened.

On those darker nights, she locked the children's door as they slept peacefully unaware of her fear, and she carried pepper spray in her pocket, just in case. Then she would pray to God to protect them all, including him, from whoever he was that night.

Visions of his mother still haunted him, driving him to desperation, and again he begged her to save herself and the children, but she would always respond in the same way, resolute in her love for him. He did not trust himself anymore.

The journey of their life continued down many paths. Most of the roads spun in endless circles, digging them deeper into their fears, leading them no where.

Still, they clung to each other. In the spinning vortex of their lives, fighting alcoholism and the prejudice levied against them by the outside world, their togetherness was their strongest weapon.

Alcoholism is a disease, not a choice, which takes down everything in its path. But it doesn't have to take away love. That is a choice. They fought it as best they could with everything that they had.

People would sometimes ask her, "How can you care about him? One minute he is sober and nice, then the next minute *he* is drunk and abusive." She would steadily say, "Because I love him and to me he is always the same." Only the wise ones understood.

The sickness was not who he truly was. It was external to his soul and his being. He was the most precious of God's children, who fights the battle of darkness within himself, without the world's support and understanding. He was a true soldier of the soul. So she stood by him, morning, noon and night, never leaving his side. When all help was exhausted, she was his help.

They had tried every external source of treatment that was available. But the ultimate truth was that was his destiny. They both knew it. He had been too damaged from the beginning by his parents and he was unable to repair that damage, though he valiantly tried. But neither one of them was willing to give up.

God in his wisdom knew the truth. It is easy to love someone when things are perfect, but love is at its best when it is being tested and it remains strong. To love unconditionally, as everyone knows, means to love someone completely as they are. Some modern romances simply end for trivial reasons. They are based on the illusion of love. These two were very different. They were on the path of the heart.

In his mind, he heard voices as she did, only they were the muttering voices of the darkness, not of the guides. They would try to coerce him to do their bidding when he was drunk. "Hurt them," they would whisper over and over again. But something deep inside his soul always stood strong against them, and though they tried, he refused to harm those that he loved.

Yet, the dark forces gathered around him like vultures to their nearly dead prey, and he was playing right into their hands with his pain, his anger and his vulnerability through his drinking.

She begged him many times to ask Christ for help, but he refused. In his agony he would reply, "Is it not enough that I have gone to every rehabilitation center and alcohol counselor in the state of Arizona?" He was tired, and he still could not forgive God and his mother for leaving him.

Though he didn't realize it, they were displaying God through their unconditional love for him. God had sent him help in the form of these three women to fight the demons of his pain. They were his life line to the higher forces and sometimes he would say to her in desperation, when he felt himself slipping away, "Don't let go."

She insulated the children as they grew, and held them all together. They continued to prosper, for their experience with the dark side had only made their faith stronger. They had learned a great lesson that many adults didn't know. Now they truly understood the pain of others first hand. They had been like their mother, only knowing love and sunshine in their growth. But when faced with fear and doubt, they began to develop unusual strengths of their own and an incredible empathy for those in need. They began to take their strengths out into the world, excelling, achieving, and helping others with a wisdom that far exceeded their years and surprised the adults around them. Jodie and Jennifer were the daughters of Astarte, and their faith shone as much in their darkest hour, as in their brightest moments. Both the cowboy, their mother and the guides were very proud of them.

It was a perfect love, though the petty world did not understand it. "I will never leave you," he said, "remember that,

117

no matter what happens." She did and held it close to her heart, like a pearl at an oyster's breast in the deepest part of the ocean, beyond man's touch and understanding.

She felt death coming, but she wasn't sure. She hoped that they would die together of old age. She asked the guides and Matheu simply said that nothing had been decided about their destiny. He would say no more, except that the resolution lay between the cowboy and his soul. She suspected that the battle with the dark forces would escalate again. So she tried to protect them all in every way she could think of. She always confiscated the car keys and kept all weapons locked up in a special gun cabinet when he was drinking. She had learned from past experience to do this. She did not know that he kept a secret, second set of keys hidden away for himself, in case of an emergency.

One day in an intense meditation she had a strange visitor. It was a woman cloaked in blue. She had dark brown hair and eyes of compassion that silently spoke in themselves.

She said in a beautiful voice, "You must have faith to survive. Your husband will be going away for a short time, but then he will be returning, healed, never to leave you again. I have come to ease your pain because of your great love for each other. I know of your struggle and how you have fought for him. My son also went away, which broke my heart and tested my faith, but his faith was stronger, and he too returned to me. May God be with you." She smiled and said her name was Mary. Then she faded from view.

The channel knew who she was, for she felt her loving energy, but she did not fully understand the meaning of the message. It perplexed her, for she could not see where he would be going and the guides would not tell her. This lesson was for him alone, and she was not to interfere in the outcome.

She had always been taught by spirit never to dictate the path of another. That path was a choice, which lay between God and the soul of an individual. She could offer help and alternatives, as she had with his drinking, but ultimately, it was his choice to stop drinking. It then became her choice to stay with him on his path. With his family beside him, he continued to face his destiny with dignity and courage, and was the best of his kind.

True evil has an intelligence. It silently waits, lulling you into complacency, then strikes like a sudden storm. That is how it claims its victims in this world.

Sometimes, he would not drink. Then he would begin drinking without incident, seemingly happy, but change at a moment's notice, like a poisonous snake striking for the kill.

They had known deep down, that his drinking would reach a crisis. It had accelerated over time damaging him. But he still refused to stop, nor could he forgive those who had hurt him.

She had been told by the guides, that he would have to make a choice between life and death. At the very least, he was killing himself slowly. She also knew that she was at risk, as long as she stayed with him. She had asked Matheu and had been told that her children would remain safe. Their destiny was to live.

She did not want to die and she did not want him to die. She knew that the soul was eternal and that his healing could come at any time, whether in this physical dimension, or, on the other side in the higher dimensions. She hoped that he would heal here and stay with her forever. She kept hoping that he would stop drinking and she kept trying to save him from himself.

She did not know how or when he would make his choice, for she was not allowed that knowledge. His life was his own.

As he drank, she tried not to focus on the darkness or on the fear, for it incapacitated her. When she grew afraid, she felt lost and powerless to help him, the children or herself, and the enemy gained strength against them all. She remained upbeat and focused on who he really was, which was a good man.

One day he wrote her a letter, for sometimes, as everyone knows, it is easier to express your feelings in words that are written rather than spoken. It said, "I know how hard it has been for you and the girls. I have tried to quit, but can't. Just know that drunk or sober I will always love you and the girls. I will always be there."

The evil weighed on him, corroding his senses through the drink, covering up his soul's essence, like a putrid blanket of smog hiding the sun, until he was left almost destroyed and starving for the light.

He was two people. The man who loved and protected her, and the demon that possessed him and wanted blood.

He turned to her after his bouts of drinking for he was afraid. She never turned away, but fed his starving heart and soul. Her love refreshed him, as rain refreshes the desert after a long drought. As the evil drained him, she restored him at her own expense, sustaining him with her own life. She still looked for ways to save him, but could find none.

The morning was beautiful. They woke up happy and loving each other as they had never before. When the darkness breaks, the light is twice as lovely, and they felt it more fully that morning than they had for a long time.

They played together all day long like children. But then the drink called him again, and late in the day, he began to drink more and more heavily, until the darkness had totally eclipsed his soul and something sinister had taken over his personality. She begged him to stop drinking that night, but he refused.

He had drunk so heavily that he felt as if he were sleepwalking. He didn't know where he was. It was pitch black in his mind, and he heard many voices telling him to shoot her. He argued with them. I can't shoot her, he thought brokenly, the words echoing like shrapnel in his mind. He didn't know what was happening to him, for it seemed more like a bad dream from which he couldn't awaken. He tried to force himself awake. He felt someone struggling with him for the gun in his hand. But the voices shouted, "Shoot!" They screamed in his mind and pounded his brain with such intensity that he thought his head would burst. "No," he whispered, "I will not hurt them." He heard the screams of the children from far away as she made them run.

He felt powerless against the forces that threatened to take them all. They were unyielding in their hold over him and his psyche was beginning to collapse in the struggle.

All of a sudden he heard a calm voice speaking over all the others. It said, "My name is Michael, come with me."

He was being ripped apart. They wouldn't let him go. He heard the cries of the children calling their mother, and his mind flashed back to his own childhood when he had lost his own mother. At that point he been condemned to die. He began to struggle even harder, for he would not condemn those children to the same fate that he had suffered.

"Shoot," they said again, "Shoot."

"Come with me," said the archangel holding out his hand.

The last image he had in his final moments was of her face and then he grasped the hand. In his mind, he was holding her hand. He pointed the gun to his head and pulled the trigger.

He saved her life that night. There were no trumpets or an angelic chorus singing hallelujah, but it was a night of majesty, for no greater love had ever existed between two people, than the channel who sacrificed everything for the cowboy, and the cowboy who sacrificed his life for her and for their children.

The battles of good and evil are always fought from within. God's unconditional love is stronger than any other force in the universe, and they were a shining example of it.

And the world went on as before. The small people grew even smaller, and gossiped, running around in circles whispering with their big mouths hanging open, trying to figure out, but unable to understand, why a girl had given up everything for a boy and a boy had shot himself. "Perhaps," they thought smugly, "He never loved her at all." The petty cannot understand the great, and never will. That is the difference between the eagle and the ant.

They had beat the devil at his own game, for he had never understood that the cowboy loved her. The devil knows nothing of love. He wanted them both, but got neither, for he was taken way beyond the devil's reach.

At the moment of his death, there was both sorrow and victory. Like a slain hero, the angels honored him for his sacrifice and prayed for her. They knew it was just the beginning, and not the end of their love.

Song of The Heavens

Like a total eclipse, darkness descended on them both, shrouding their eyes with the pain of separation that only mortal death could bring and neither could bear.

In her world, the morning sun rose on schedule, illuminating the mountains and the desert, but she neither saw nor felt it, for her eyes were veiled by his death and her soul was cloaked by an indescribable sorrow that only the light of his eyes could lift. Both were blinded by his death.

His body lay lifeless in a pool of blood and his eyes were dark. It was as if all light had left the world, for the light of his eyes shining was the source of the light of her life.

She heard the pitter patter of many feet tending their inevitable tasks around her, but the sounds were hollow and empty, for none echoed with the music of the silver bell spurs that he always wore. The bells were silent, and with that silence there was no hope. Faith faded into despair and she could not go on without him.

He had not intended to end his life. Something greater had forced his hand into a choice. His drunkenness and his anger had rendered him vulnerable and he had fallen prey to a deeper darkness than his own, which had been stalking them both.

He was worn, for he had been fighting this battle his whole life and it seemed that he had no more strength left. Yet, in that one moment, he drew upon his heart more fully than ever before to discover the truth.

She had always known the truth of his heart, despite his doubts and the doubts of the rest of the world. And a greater heart could not be found. He had found his faith through loving her. He was her hero and a child of God.

Matheu wept for them both, as he stood helplessly by her, invisible, immortal, yet unable to change the course of the tide which had swept them both away. He tried to ease the shock and the pain with the warmth of his loving energy, knowing the boy's guides were doing the same for him. Their legacy came from a much higher place and was beyond the control of the guides.

As he stood there beside her, he remembered ages past. A faithful girl, both frightened and fearless, had led an army to crown a faithless boy king. She had given her life for her faith. Today that young boy, who had never fully understood that faith, had finally accepted and embraced it through his love for her. Michael had led them both times. Such was the karma of their souls of which they were unaware.

As the bullet went into his head, he felt no fear or pain, for he was carried by a giant wave of love, stronger than his fear of death, into the higher dimensions of time.

An explosion and a blinding flash of light engulfed his brain, as he literally spilled out of his body and was washed away in the tide of past, present and future time. Somehow, he felt strong hands guiding him past dangerous currents that would drown him if they could. The coroner claimed his body, but the river of eternal life carried his soul safely to the shores of the higher vibrations, to a different place of existence where all time is one.

Then all conscious thought left him, as he surrendered control over to whatever force was carrying him. He woke up spinning, still half drunk and dazed, not remembering what had happened. He felt as if he had been run through a wringer. He looked around him to get his hearings. He was in the desert, sprawled by a blazing campfire. He could not see clearly in the distance. It appeared to be dusk or dawn, for even though there was a sense of dimness, the air sparkled with light. He tried, but could not remember how *he* got there.

He knew he must have had another blackout. During those times, he could do or say anything and not remember a thing. He thought perhaps that he had wandered there on his own sometime during the night and had passed out again while he was drunk. He had never seen this place before. The air seemed different. He didn't realize that he was dead. He still existed in mortal form, though he felt very strange. He didn't even suspect that he was dead, for to him death meant non existence, or, as he had put it many times before, meat for the worms.

After a short while, he began to panic, for he could not figure out where he was and how to get home. He began to worry that something terrible had happened to his family, or if it hadn't, they would be terrified by his disappearance.

There was a strange buzzing within him and around him, as if he were in some sort of electrical field. He felt cold despite this energy and sick to his stomach. The fear rose in him, that he wanted to go home from this strange place, to where he was loved and warm and safe. He wanted the warmth of his wife most of all.

All of a sudden, he came out of nowhere. He looked like an old time prospector, who had been panning for gold, with his comfortably worn clothes and a long full beard. Silently, he walked slowly up to the campfire carrying a blanket, which he handed to the cowboy, who sat shivering on the ground. The cowboy gratefully accepted it and wrapped himself, though it seemed to be of little use as the coldness was coming from within him.

The man's eyes were brilliantly lit as he gazed down at the boy in a grandfatherly sort of way, which somehow comforted the young man. He felt better in this kindly old man's presence, and at least now he was not alone. He thought perhaps this old man could help him find his way home.

His voice was like velvet, deep in tone as he spoke, introducing himself. He said his name was Victor, and he was a guide in those parts. After a brief pause, Victor gently told him what had happened. Victor said that he was dead and that he could not go home as he had come, for his physical body was useless. He told him that the body he felt around him was his ethereal body and of a different substance than his physical body.

The cowboy's head was spinning. He did not believe him. The buzzing around him seemed to grow more intense. He began to feel dizzy, like he was losing his grip on reality. He became very angry and began to argue with the old man, who sat impassively as the boy vented his wrath. The old man repeated his message, until the boy finally said, "You must be crazy old man. I am going home, no matter what you say. How can I be dead if I'm sitting here with you?"

The old man sat thoughtfully for a moment. "I'll take you home," he said. "Close your eyes and remember, thoughts are reality. Focus on your wife and home." The cowboy hesitated, then shut his eyes in desperation and thought of home. Suddenly, they were in his living room, and there she was sitting silently on the couch, grief stricken and alone. He could see everything very clearly. But she could not see them, for grief had grounded her vibration with its heavy weight, and they were at a light vibration much higher than the physical. He tried to comfort her, but she could not feel him, for she was numb from the pain and he was made of energy, not of flesh.

He was devastated, for he could not reach her. She did not know that he was still alive, but in a different place and time. She seemed not to know anything, for grief had stripped her of her life energy as it had stripped him of his life. He didn't know what to do to help her or himself.

Victor told him softly that he had to go away to heal himself, for he had been very damaged on the physical plane and then he could decide what to do with his destiny. She would do the same in her world and the decision would be made after they both had recovered from the shock. He said that no decisions would be made for them, as God's gift to all souls was the free will to create their own destiny. At this time, they were both too weak to understand their choices and to make that commitment.

The cowboy felt trapped. Like a wounded wild animal, he was ready to attack anyone who got in his way. Defiantly, he told the guide to go to Hell, or wherever it was that he came from and insisted that he wasn't going away anywhere. He told the guide that if there was a God, which he had yet to see, then he could just fix things. He told the guide that he loved her more than anything and he wasn't going to lose her.

Victor smiled, for he understood the nature of love and loyalty better than the boy knew. He had expected this, for he knew the circumstances of his death, yet he was still amazed by the boy's refusal to leave her. Most souls willingly go down their path like sheep, looking for a leader to follow. These two were very different. They were leaders.

To calm him, Victor attempted to explain the situation more clearly. He told him that his wife was in linear time on the physical plane. Linear time, which was created by mankind based upon the illusion of limitations, runs slowly forward, one moment after the other in succession. He explained that people in body think they can only do one thing at a time. The cowboy however, having left his body and the physical plane through death, had also left the illusion of linear time behind and entered into the realm of universal time, or timelessness, which is circular, and is where all moments, past, present and future come into one. This meant that he could do many things at the same time. He told the cowboy that all time is one in all the dimensions, but the physical body limits mankind's vision through the illusion of barriers which do not exist. He explained to the boy that he would soon experience this phenomenom, if he would allow himself the opportunity to do so without creating those same barriers in his mind. He could heal and stay with his wife at the same time.

"Where the hell am I?" the cowboy asked.

"You are currently in the sixth dimension, which is the entry level for souls upon death, according to their individual circumstances and conditions. Some souls proceed to higher levels. Children have a level of their own, to heal in and to proceed with their growth at an accelerated rate. But, you are at the beginning, in the closest dimension to the physical plane."

"The fifth and the fourth dimensions, though not physical dimensions, are still connected with the earth plane in a gradual reduction of psychic energy to the solidity of the third and physical dimension. Ideas are formed in the fourth and the fifth dimensions. They are not a solid world, but a land of dreams. Mankind can elevate their energy to the level of the fourth and the fifth dimensions with great ease, though most are completely unaware of it. Great thinkers, writers and inventors have already done this and in doing so have recognized universal time, for they are doing two things or more, at once. They are creating in that space, while still functioning in the physical and third dimension. Worldly psychics read the future by elevating their energy to the fourth and the fifth dimensions and that is why their predictions fluctuate. They are not rising above the world of dreams, but getting caught up in them, reading them as fact, when simply they are nothing more than a part of the same illusion, and may, or may not happen. Some souls in transition choose to stay there, caught in the web of the fantasy. But you made it safely through to solid ground. Therefore, the fourth and the fifth dimensions or the astral plane, as some call it, is a world of illusion and dreams still connected with the physical."

"But all souls are multidimensional, and capable of living in many dimensions at the same time. Most people on the physical plane shrink themselves in fear and negativity, creating more barriers in their mind. In truth, they are forgetting that they are already multidimensional souls temporarily experiencing the physical body, who have the same power in the physical as they do in the ethereal. They instead believe they must wait until physical death removes their limitations. They think, this is all that there is and I must wait until I die to find the answers and to be set free. They already have the answers within themselves, though they are blinded to that, trapped in the illusions of the physical reality and the barriers in their own minds. They want God to remove these barriers, giving them freedom, but they must do it for themselves on all levels, even here, though assistance will be provided if genuinely requested. God has already given them the power to free themselves. But they are afraid of what they will find, so they hold on to what they know, limiting themselves in fear, instead of expanding themselves in freedom and unconditional love."

"But your wife is different. It is true that she is temporarily unaware and blinded by her pain, but she will awaken very soon to who she is. She is a channel, which you should already know."

"She has elevated her energy to dimensions beyond this one and has sat in council with guides other than myself. She has lived the multidimensionality of the soul. She has the ability to communicate with you."

"You see, most people in the physical look for answers outside themselves. They think eternity and salvation lie outward. They look for their Creator in the outer world, not realizing that what they will find is nothing more than an illusion that is self created, and is limited by their inner world. Until they realize that all truth lies within, their outer world will not change but continue in chaos, for it is merely a reflection of what they believe and hold within themselves. All lies within, and the outside world is simply a mirror of one's inner world."

"You wife knows this, and if you will let me, I will help you to remove the barriers from your own mind. This will enable you to communicate with her, as soon as you both are able. Then and only then, can you begin to discuss your future plans. This is the first and the only step you can take in going home. Later on, there may be other steps. But this step will open the door to those and enable you to tell her that you are all right and have survived."

The cowboy was confused and frightened. He understood some of the things, but had not heard what he wanted to hear. A part of him still denied his own death. He had gone away many times before physically, to another state, or another town, but he was always able to go home. Now, he was in a different dimension and a different time. He didn't know how he would find his way back. He wanted to be in the same time and the same place as his wife, not in some Twilight Zone, with a batty old man. But having no other choice, he allowed the guide to take his unwilling arm. In doing so, he began his long journey home, though at the time, he felt more lost than ever.

In the blink of an eye, they found themselves in a small room that resembled a library, with a large book upon a wooden table. The book was bound in leather and etched in gold. The cowboy stared around him with great fascination. Then reality hit him and he remembered his wife. In an instant, with that memory, he found he was there with her in the same room. It was as if this study was without walls and interconnected with their living room at home, whose walls had also vanished, though at a distance. Both rooms were merged together in the same space, so

129

he could be in the study with Victor, and in the living room with her at the same time. "How is this possible?" he asked the guide.

"Remember, all things interconnect, and all time and space are one," said the guide, "Now, you will read about yourself and your wife, and the history of your souls and their relationship together. That is the best way to understand what is happening and to prepare yourself for what is coming, so you can help her to accept and to understand it also, for she will need your guidance more than ever."

In his lifetime he had never read anything more than stories of the Old West, but he began to read, desperately seeking the answer to his questions on how to find his way back home. It seemed as if he read forever about his wife, himself, and the story of their souls, which stretched back farther than he could ever imagine. He felt as if they were characters in a story book, as different identities, times and places played out in his mind like a never ending movie.

But there was a part of him that was always aware of her presence in the living room of their home, which was within his vision at the same time and in the same room he was in. At first it was difficult for him to do two things at once, and he would constantly interrupt the story in his mind to look at her and to make sure she was still there. But after awhile, all thoughts just flowed together in him and he found that he could see her at the same time he visualized the story he was reading in his mind. This was not an easy feat, for he was still in the beginning stages of transformation. But his determination not to lose sight of her was so strong, that nothing could deter him. He was afraid that she would fade away, so he kept a constant and vigilant eye on her.

And he also found that by watching her, he could better keep a grip on himself and who he was, for he was afraid of losing himself in the changing circumstances. Other identities and personalities leaped at him from the pages, coming to life in his mind, until he felt that he was losing his sanity as to what was real and what was not. To protect himself and to protect his family, he tried to keep a singular purpose in mind. And that was going home, as the same person he was when he left there. So he

130

went along with things, as long as they did not interfere with that purpose of being himself and staying connected to her.

At the same time, a new side began to emerge within him, as he read more and more about their various incarnations. He was like a diamond in the rough that was beginning to shine with many different facets. He was especially intrigued by those lifetimes that involved the Old West, and he asked Victor many questions about reincarnation and how it worked. It seemed to be an individual soul's choice, which the soul did at his own pace, or not at all, for you can learn wherever you are. The soul either did it alone, or in partnership with other souls. They had always been together in one way or another. He began to see a pattern and thought silently to himself that if they had always been together, then they could find a way never to be apart again. Perhaps reincarnation is the answer, he thought. He tried to find the future pages of the book, but they were blank. Victor explained that the future had not yet been decided by them, and that the pages were being written even as they spoke. The book was called The Book of All Souls, and contained all records pertaining to them. No further information was made available to him, for he had many decisions to make and he had to make them on his own, the guide explained.

Victor explained that his soul was porous and made of energy so that the information just drifted in quite naturally, almost by osmosis, and that there was no need to struggle for it. It was easily accessed and immediately available, if he would just let it happen.

The cowboy still had his same physical form, but he felt much lighter, as if he were draining and becoming emptier. The guide told him that was a part of the natural process of releasing the flesh and that it would take time to complete. He explained that the ethereal body of light resembles the molecular structure of the physical, but is less dense, and his was still attached to his physical body with invisible threads, which would slowly break within the next few days, completely freeing his soul.

So like a snake shedding his skin, unwillingly, but without any choice in the matter, he began his transition from mortal man to spirit, while still clinging to his life and to his wife, whom he adamantly refused to leave behind. His reality was changing, yet he held on to the one thing that would never change and that he could count on, which was her. It kept away the panic and fed his faith that somehow, someway, everything would be all right.

The initial excitement over his new found abilities began to wear off and with his head still spinning from the effects of the transition itself and with the new information that was pouring uncontrolled into his being, he began to tire. Victor explained that at that lower level of development, his soul had limited energy. It would increase over time and he would find less of a need to sleep or to seek sustenance.

"Is there any beer here?" the boy asked.

"We have only one drink here and you may flavor it as you wish. It will cleanse you during the process of transition, and restore the vitality to your being. I think you may find that it resembles your water. It is the same with our food. It is the manna of our existence and though you may form it and experience it in any way you wish, in essence, it is only bread."

Bread and water, the cowboy thought to himself, I am getting the hell out of here.

The guide laughed uproariously, as if the boy's thoughts were spoken. "Remember, JJ, thoughts are reality," he said, and taking the boy's arm, they found themselves in a small room, with a wooden bed and a chair. A white garment was draped over the chair. The bedroom resembled a monk's cell in its bareness and simplicity. As he thought of home, it interconnected with the space of his living room and his wife, who sat forlornly in it. The guide then left him to rest and to assimilate what he had been through.

So he sat alone in that chair in the sixth dimension, feeling more pain than he thought he could ever feel, as his former self seemed to slowly drain away. And she sat alone in the third dimension, in such grief, terror and mortal agony, that he feared she would harm herself. She was completely unaware that *he* was watching her.

He desperately wanted a drink, but there was no more alcohol and he didn't want water. He wanted to hold her, but he couldn't, because he didn't know how and she couldn't feel him anyway. She couldn't save him anymore as she always had, for she could not see him and what had truly happened. It was up to him to save them both and he vowed that he would.

He swore to God that he would do anything if only he could break the icy spell that separated them, so they could be together in the warmth of their love again.

It seemed like forever that he was sitting there in that chair on the other side of time, afraid to move for fear his home would fade away. There was no escaping the reality that he had created. He couldn't use her to avoid himself or to ease his feelings, which were building within him. He certainly did not feel immortal. If anything, he felt more mortal and vulnerable than ever before. He felt small and scared compared to the universe which had taken control of his life.

His feelings were becoming magnified in this new energy and harder to deny. He had always been able to deny them before. But here that seemed impossible. He had never allowed himself to be as full of feelings as he was in those moments. He couldn't seem to control them and they were like giant waves in that turbulent ocean of himself, threatening to drown him. He was exhausted from the experience of trying to subdue them. He had always been able to control them before through drinking. He did not have superhuman strength, just superhuman sensitivity and he thought it ironic that death had made him feel more alive instead of less. Dead men do cry, he thought.

As *he* stared at her in desperation, struggling with his own pain, he could almost see the cloud of grief surrounding her, weighing her down as if the mountains themselves had fallen on her and were crushing her to death. She was weak from not eating or sleeping. Like a prisoner in a cell, her only sustenance was not bread and water, like his, but coffee and cigarettes.

The children came to him in his peripheral vision. They seemed frightened and worried about their mother. It was almost as if they were afraid she would vanish too. They tiptoed through the house as if on a mine field, not wanting to do anything that might awaken the demons again. She didn't seem to notice, so lost was she in her own pain.

After awhile, he started to remember the times they had been through together, and found that by doing so, he felt a little bit better. Memories and thoughts came vibrantly alive in his mind, as if he were reliving them and she were there by his side again. It seemed to ease the pressure that he was feeling and made him feel closer to her, so he continued his journey through time in his mind, down the roads of the past which had brought them together.

Without the effects of the alcohol which had clouded his vision and the darkness which had invaded his heart, he could see more clearly than ever before. Whenever he thought of an event he would almost be swallowed whole, for it would surround him and fill his senses with the full experience, almost as if it were really happening again and they were a part of it. With this experience, he began to understand the expression, all time is one. And he marvelled at the recognition that he was here in the present, but was experiencing the past more fully than he had when it happened before.

He did not know it at the time, but he begun a process which would take him years to complete. It was an independent review of his life, brought about by the feelings he was experiencing. This was required of all souls in crossing over, but was never assigned, for it was part of the natural order of things and the transition itself. It just happened at one's own pace. He was not being forced, but felt the need within himself. There was no external judgement, only a personal desire to understand himself, his life, and what had brought him to that very place on that very day.

He began to notice a pattern in his behavior that had been repeated throughout the years since his mother had abandoned him. Anger, blame and then running away to start all over again, to repeat the same abandonment with a different person. He had never been able to forgive his mother, finding it easier to perpetuate that one action instead of facing it and healing it. His mother had only left him once, but he had relived that experience a thousand times over, brought on by his perpetual anger and his blame. He had always run away from self examination, for he did not want to face what he thought were his own shortcomings.

Deep down, he saw he didn't really blame his mother, but himself. It was almost as if he felt he had done something wrong as a small child, or he wasn't good enough and that is why she threw him away. So instead of facing his shame, he blamed her and others, to distract attention from what he thought were his own failures. He was ashamed, so he hid behind his behavior to protect himself. This way, no one would ever know the truth and be able to throw him away again. He wouldn't let them, for he would throw everyone and everything away first.

He had become an outcast in the world, for he had created that reality through his own actions. Friends, family, and society didn't want him because of his drinking, which came from his anger and his pain. No one had ever seen past that illusion into the truth of his heart until he met her.

She was the only one and she had never left him, no matter what and he had tested her. To her he was a good man. He remembered what she had said one sunny day while riding, when he was particularly down on himself. "Out of all the souls I know in the universe, to me, you are the best." And she had meant it, and she had never run from him, but only to him, though he had hurt her at times and then was sorry. She had always forgiven him and accepted it as a consequence of his life, not as who he was, for there was a difference and she could see the difference. She had tried to get him to see it for himself. She had tried to heal him through her own heart by loving him. He had never left her, only hiding at times, because she was the only one who knew him for who he truly was and loved him despite his pain and the consequences of his anger.

Life with an alcoholic had not been easy for her. He had never seen it from her point of view, for the disease had clouded his perspective. It had not been easy for him either, for in being with her he had begun to feel love again, which is what he had feared the most.

He was amazed at the sacrifices she and the children had made to stay with him. They had lost their home and financial security, family and friends had ridiculed and judged them, and they had even risked their lives, for in a drunken stupor, he could have hurt them without even knowing it. He had never before seen this so clearly, having been drunk and angry most of the time. He had never wanted to see it, for in doing so he would have to face himself, and his anger and his pain. She had even risked her clarity as a channel to stay with him, which had been the gift of her life, along with her children. To him, these were revelations and with his new found knowledge, he loved her more than ever before, as the door to his heart opened wider through the understanding. It felt like being in love for the first time, he thought, but he couldn't tell her yet. Now, he was even more determined to find a way back home.

As he watched her, he could hear the silent prayer in her mind echoing in his. Cowboy, I love you, please don't leave me behind. He thought almost reverently, with all that she has been through, she would do it all over again. He vowed never to leave her and from that moment forward, he became her first knight in life and in death.

He went back like a dragon slayer to his childhood and saw the horrible damage done to him as a young boy when his mother had left him. He realized that he had done nothing wrong. She had left him from her own pain and anger. Her pain and her anger had existed before his birth, from her own childhood and was then perpetuated into his. It became their family legacy, handed down from parent to child, generation to generation, and was like a avalanche crashing down the hill of life, getting bigger over the years and crushing everything along the way. He and his mother had been only a part of what it had crushed. He learned that pain, anger and fear have a life of their own and only unconditional love can stop them from destroying the world.

He was for the first time, experiencing time travel by going backwards and reliving those experiences. It almost felt as if he had changed things just by doing that, for he began to heal inside. There was no judgement, just incorporation into his very being on what he was learning. Sometimes, what he learned was very different from what he had thought before, for as everyone knows it is hard to see things clearly when you are right in the middle of them.

But he found that in that room alone, except for the supportive vision of his wife giving him strength, it was easier than it had ever been to face things. This gave him hope for the first time that he could heal. He did it as much for her as for himself.

In doing so, he began to develop a deeper understanding of himself and others. He finally took the first step towards forgiving himself and those that had wronged him. He found that he had a more compassionate nature than he thought.

But she had always known that and would tease him about being soft boiled, with his hard shell protecting his soft insides. And out of all the things he saw and learned, one thing stood out and that was her.

Feeling full of love and compassion for the first time in his life, he began to pray without thinking. It was not a professional prayer for no one was telling him he had to pray or what to say. It was not a prayer born out of fear, for he was unafraid. It came straight from his heart and the new love that had begun to bloom there.

It was not for himself, but for his wife and their children, for he considered them to be his children, even though genetically they were not. But the heart knows nothing of heredity, but forms its own truths. He prayed to ease their suffering and for another chance to be with them again. He prayed to make a difference in their lives from that day forward and to undo some of the damage that he had done to them. And above all, he prayed the same prayer that she was praying, which was not to leave each other behind in a universe that could swallow both of them whole in its vastness.

He didn't know it, but the guides were silently watching them both through their mind's eye, and as everyone knows, God is everwhere.

He began to grow very tired and the thought of sleep seemed very inviting. Death was certainly different than what he thought it would be. It had not been an ending of his problems at all. It had not brought him instant peace or instant answers to the issues that had plagued him his whole life. If anything, it was a continuation of the same, only at a different level and intensity, which further complicated everything.

He didn't know what would happen if he just layed down and closed his eyes. Maybe, he would wake up back home with her. His energy was fading very quickly and he felt more human than ever before. Do dead men sleep, he wondered to himself? He thought he would just lay down on the bed for a few minutes to rest and was amazed that within a minute or two, she did the same on their couch in the living room, with the dogs beside her. Within a few minutes, both of them had drifted off to an unencumbered sleep, where they seemed connected and at peace in the astral plane of dreams.

When he awoke he was still dead and still in the barren room. Nothing had changed, much to his frustration. She was still sleeping and he wished he could cover her with a blanket, for she looked cold and alone on the couch.

Victor returned from nowhere startling him. He was holding a glass of liquid in his hand. "Think your flavor," he said. Somewhat suspiciously, the cowboy thought strawberry, as he accepted the drink. It was cool and refreshing and tasted somewhat of fresh strawberries. He found it strengthened his spirit and was revitalizing to his energy. Somewhat like coffee in the morning without the buzz, he thought, but it left him clear headed and seemed to wash away some of his inner wounds.

The guide sat down in the chair and started to speak. "You will be staying here in the sixth dimension, to undergo a process of self healing. In time, you will learn to remove the conflicts from your mind that are preventing you from becoming who you truly are, which is a wonderful individual, whole within yourself and a part of the network of life."

"In physical form you were broken down into fragmented pieces of pain, fear and love, and were unable to put them together to save yourself. The drinking accelerated your death. It is true, if not for the drinking, you would still be alive, though fragmented. The drinking allowed a greater darkness to invade your soul. You lost control of yourself to that darkness. But the drinking was born of a deeper pain, which was part of the pattern of your life. Here you may safely address that deeper pain. There is much hope, for you are already aware of the love within you, as you have so courageously displayed in the final moments of your earthly life."

"During this initial process of healing, you will learn that thoughts are reality. You have the ability to create your own reality and to take responsibility for that creation. You have always had that ability, even in physical form. But the reality you created on the earth plane was a destructive one, colored by your anger and your pain. It was very difficult for you to get past those strong emotions into the feeling of love. Here, it will be easier for you."

"Think of what you have already created. You have already reestablished the bond with your wife, even though at this time she is unaware of it. Though it is just a visual bond, it can go further. You have also flavored your drink. And you have traveled in time with the essence of your mind to begin healing yourself. You have already grown. This is only the beginning of what is possible."

"As you get stronger, you can create your own surroundings, and you may choose and will be allowed to leave this room to create a better one. Or perhaps a house, or whatever else suits you. Your potential is truly unlimited on whatever you wish to create. It has always been unlimited. But on the earth plane, where you are caught up in the illusion, you become a part of it. It is somewhat like mass hysteria, where people believe in what they see, instead of creating their own reality."

"Your mother taught you that you were unworthy of love. You believed that you were unworthy of love. Filled with that pain, others around you responded to it and treated you as if you were unworthy of love. Only one person did not respond to that illusion and that was your wife. She saw the truth about you and tried to break the illusion so that you could see the truth about yourself. This would have started you on the road to healing. If the walls of that bitter illusion had come tumbling down, you would have found yourself surrounded by much love."

"The illusion created by you and many others judging you was a distorted vision of yourself. Somewhat like a mirror that exaggerated your features from man to monster. You began to live the distortion. She saw you not as a monster, but as the man that you truly were. But you yourself were afraid to make the transformation, to let go of the anger and the pain, for fear of becoming vulnerable. It was safer to remain a monster in the world's eyes, then to be a vulnerable man, as she knew you truly were."

"Here you have no other choice. To progress beyond here, you must face yourself. But remember, all is an illusion which comes from within. The truth lies within your own heart, not without. That is why people face daily what lies within themselves. They look outward for solutions, when the answer lies inward. Unless they are willing to go within themselves to remove the excess layers from their beings, which cover their true selves, they will only find in their lives a reflection of that which covers them. It will be a reflection of the distortion of who they are, instead of who they truly are. Nothing will change for them until it changes from within. And that is true in any dimension. Outer life is only a reflection of what lies within. Your wife knew that and struggled to create a better image of worth within you, that you might get in touch with your true self. But it is something that you must do for yourself or it will not work."

"In time you will remove some of those layers which cover your heart. In fact, you have already begun. You have a wonderful heart. But you seem to think that you do not and you use those layers as an armor, protecting you from what you fear you will find, to shield yourself from more pain. But instead, you deny yourself the love that you seek, that would finally free you from the pain that you have suffered and from the fear of it happening again. You have not been able to do this in the physical and as in the physical you must choose to do it here. In a sense you have already chosen that road, for you have begun reviewing your life from a different and more compassionate perspective. That is the first step on the long road of healing, which will make you whole again and at peace with yourself and the greater universe. It is the first step in coming closer to your wife and to God."

"Remember, you have brought with you the same issues that you have left your lifetime with. Your outer world is still but a reflection of your inner world. Nothing has changed, but the circumstances surrounding you. You may deal with these issues at your own pace. Nothing will be forced. But unless you do, you cannot evolve from this dimension. You must face yourself here at this level of the light, which is more intense than the physical plane, but, of a lesser intensity than the other dimensions. Here you can freely visit places and periods of time, which will enable you to make a decision from a clearer perspective on your place in the universe, where you have come from and where you are going."

"All souls go through a period of dormancy and self examination before they embark on a new stage of growth, for they must heal from their previous incarnation, understanding and integrating what they have learned, resolving all conflict and all unfinished business, before they are free to embark on any other future course. Some souls may chose never to reincarnate, but remain evolving in the higher dimensions."

"There is no rush, you have all the time that you need, for this is a timeless environment. For some, it may take a very long time for their lifetimes have been very turbulent and they have a lot of damage to repair to themselves and to others. You are held responsible for what you have done. For others, it may be very brief, for they have already begun this process during their lifetimes, which accelerates their growth. Either way, no soul may progress to the higher dimensions of truth and light, until they have resolved those inner issues that are preventing them from being one with themselves, with their brethren, and with God their Creator."

"As one progresses beyond this level to the dimensions leading to completion, the light and the truth become much more intense and the energy for creation greater. For some that process may take an eternity to realize, for souls that are not ready for that elevation would only destroy themselves within that intensity. For others it may only be a moment. But until you have mastered the responsibility of the basic energy here, you cannot progress to a higher dimension for it would be too dangerous. It

141

would be like giving dynamite to a child. Instead, the child must build with clay first. Think of it in terms of your earthly schools. We, as children of God, must complete one grade successfully before we can be promoted to a higher grade or dimension of creation."

"How you choose to live in this dimension is up to you. When you first arrived, you found yourself in front of a campfire. There was no campfire there before and there is not one there now. That illusion was created by your soul for your own comfort. Others who make the transition may find themselves in another illusion, such as being greeted by loved ones. Some who have created nothing but hell for themselves and for others on earth, will find themselves in an illusion of that inner hell."

"You have not completely released the physical yet, which you will do within the next five days of linear time. After that is complete and as you acclimate to your new situation, you are free to do here as you wish. I am your guide and will help you all that I can."

"At this level you will have a limited amount of energy that will gradually increase. You will still need to rest and to take sustenance, somewhat as you did before. This will diminish over time. As you progress in the higher dimensions, there is no need for that. Here you may form your own body and clothing with your own thoughts. In the higher dimensions, you will not feel the need to form a physical body at all to exist. These are things that you will learn by experiencing them. Together, we may create a better reality than you have ever thought possible. What you do with that is up to you. It is even possible to form friendships here, if you open yourself to them. But that also, is up to you. No one is forced to do anything against their will. I am only allowed to assist you, the rest you must do for yourself. Ultimately, your future is in your own hands and your destiny lies between you and the God that created you."

The cowboy was stunned. He had been hoping against hope that things would change by themselves. He was really a dead man who couldn't go home. He wanted his real life back, the freedom of the ride, the fire of the beer in his belly, the warmth of his home and the loving heart of his wife. "But what about my family," he pleaded, "They have bills to pay, and the horses to take care of. They need me."

He left something else unspoken. There was a rising fear in the pit of his stomach that threatened to overwhelm him. He was afraid to heal. Here, he couldn't run away. He had avoided facing himself his whole life and he wanted to avoid it again. He felt that he had done enough healing by reviewing his life in those few moments. It was time to get back to reality as he knew it. He had learned his lesson. He wanted to go home and maintain things as they were. The boy forgot that his thoughts were easily read.

The guide sat silent for a moment and then smiled. "You have fooled everyone in your lifetime, except for perhaps your wife, who accepted you and loved you unconditionally, even though she knew what would happen to her if she did. She has an exceptional guide. But you cannot fool me. I know you are afraid, and your cunning simply hides that fear. It is easier for you to live with what you have already created, than to face your fear, heal it and then to create something better. But it is too late to return as you came. Here, you will he safe while healing. That is the only way you can help yourself, and ultimately her."

"Your physical body is dead and your energy, which is your soul, would be repelled by it magnetically, should you attempt to reenter it. You cannot enter a vessel that is broken. Think of it this way. Your body was like a bottle that held the fluid essence of your soul. Upon your physical death, the bottle cracked, releasing that fluid essence. If you tried to enter it again, you would spill out, for a cracked vessel can no longer hold it's fluid. You will soon see that your wife will begin to prepare the proper arrangements to care for your body and you may view and participate in that if you wish."

The boy stared at the sleeping form of his wife, choking back tears. Clearing the panic from his throat, he turned to the guide and said, "But what of her? She won't make it without me. You must know that if you know everything. Look at her," he said, the anger rising in his voice. "This is not her fault. But she is suffering because of me. I have seen a lot of things here that I didn't know were possible. There must be a way. We need each other."

With great compassion, Victor placed his hand over the cowboy's and said, "It is true. Because of your death, she may not survive. Her future, like yours, is not written in stone, but is created as you go. All time and space are one to the soul and the lesson may be completed in the physical or beyond. God gives everyone the free will and the power to create anything they wish. Sometimes, the illusion created is a negative and a destructive one, resulting in situations like this. Sometimes it is a positive one. Either way, you have created this and you must live with it."

"In reality, you are not separate from her. You are both in the same room, are you not? All that lacks is her awareness, which may or may not change over time. If you are aware of her and she is aware of you, then you are somewhat together, but in a different way."

"But I want to be together with her in the same way as before," the cowboy responded.

"That is no longer possible," Victor said, "Your adult male physical body is dead. Yet, you do have another option that I will explain to you, now that you are better prepared to understand it. Every being that has died before completing his life lessons has a short amount of time to reincarnate back into physical form to complete those lessons. It is true, you and she were meant to be physically together. However, you would have to be reborn into the world as an infant, starting from the very beginning of the life cycle to continue this process. You would be born with exactly the same problems that you had when you left and you would be facing the same dilemmas, which are that of abandonment, resulting in anger and alcoholism. The ending would be up to you, for even though the blueprint would be the same, the circumstances would be different. You have six months of linear time in which to make this decision."

"Would I be born to her?" the boy asked in confusion.

"The circumstances of your birth would not be of your choosing. There are higher forces that would decide what would ultimately be best for both of you in that regard. However, it is

144

highly likely that because both of you desire so greatly to be reunited in the flesh, that this would occur. It is possible that you would be born to her, if she desired it, asked for it, and facilitated it through her physical actions. She would have to be an active participant in this creation. Or, you would enter her life through an outside source, such as the child of a friend, or a family member. You could even be her grandchild. Your bond is with her and you would make your way back to her physically in some way to continue that bond. But this could only be done with her permission and the genuine desire which comes from her heart. It is the same with you. That is how reality is created. Your karmic bond would then continue in the physical. But remember, it would not be the same. You would not be her husband, but her child. The entire burden would be placed upon her to raise you. Upon reincarnation, your consciousness would be washed clean and you would have no memory of your former life, even though you would bear the same characteristics. You would be a different person. You would not be you. She would not know for certain that it was you returning to her in infant form and this would plague her. She would die eventually, when you are very young and again you would lose her and become embittered by it, facing the same issues of abandonment all over again, but in a different way. Either way, whether you stay here, or return as an infant, you must face and resolve these issues."

"Can I not go back as a man and be her husband?" he asked poignantly.

"You cannot go back as a full grown man. You cannot just walk into another man's body. It is not allowed. You have been given one body in this lifetime and you have lost it. You must heal yourself here, before you can proceed with your growth, or if you so wish, you may return to the physical as a newborn, and try to resolve your problems there. But I must warn you. If you return to the physical in the state that you are in, you will suffer greatly again and you will eventually drink to ease that suffering. It will be the same thing all over again for you. It will complicate a matter which is already greatly complicated. And she will not know for certain where you are and that will destroy her."

The cowboy's eyes filled with tears and he sobbed, "I cannot do this without her."

"Listen to me," the guide said, "Nothing has been decided. Your wife seems to be embarking upon a course of willful death, which is not unlike your suicide, but is a slow wasting away of her mind and her body. She has lost the will to live and is letting go. She has not yet decided if she will survive. So closely aligned are your souls, you are like one being. She feels as if a part of her has already died with your passing and she may not be strong enough to continue. She has been so weakened throughout the years of your disease and so traumatized with your death, that it is highly unlikely that she will find the will to go on. In reality, if she does survive, she would not be the same as before and she would find herself alone and unable to reach her full potential of growth. She was meant to be her own namesake, which is that of spreading joy to others. That was her work and that was her training. But she has been broken, as you were and nothing short of a miracle can restore her to what she was before that night. Nothing can give back to her what was taken from her heart, for you cannot go back as her husband, which is the only thing that she wants and would heal her completely at this point."

"I can't let this happen," the cowboy said. "Is there nothing I can do to save her as she saved me?"

"She must be willing to save herself," the guide answered. "But you can help her find her faith again through your love, as she has done for you. From here, you can still heal together. You can communicate this to her, letting her know that you still love her and that you wish to continue with her, but in a different way. As I have said before, remember who she is. She is an unusual woman with unusual abilities and this situation is one of a kind. The impossible becomes possible through unyielding commitment. Your continuing commitment to each other opens the door to many possibilities."

"You see, in the beginning, God created a universe undivided. There was no separation, for all time and space are one. But mankind chose it through their belief systems and created it through their behavior. These chasms have affected the

146

entire network of life. Unity can only be restored by changing those beliefs through faith and unconditional love. This in itself, would be a new beginning for all."

"You see, most beings, when they pass from the physical plane to the spirit plane in the manner they call death, go through a period of reflection and yearning for what they have left behind. It is a grieving time. After that period is over and the feelings lessen, they adjust to their new situations and begin creating new bonds in which to comfort themselves. They willingly let go. They have new lives and even though they love those that they have left behind, they are not truly commited to anything but themselves and what they need to further their own growth. They have neither the skill, nor the desire to learn the skills needed to maintain a bond with those that remain on the physical plane. Nor do those in the physical have the skill or the desire to learn those skills needed to maintain a bond with their loved ones in another dimension. For all purposes, they too, after a grieving period, move on with their lives. To maintain such a bond, takes much work and commitment, and ultimately, a special kind of love. You and she have that love and that ability, for you have moved together as one being in life. Now, even in death and transformation, that is possible."

"I don't want to grow apart and fade away from her and I don't want to be her child. I want to be her husband. I didn't want to end my marriage that night. This is all a mistake. I didn't mean to shoot myself. I didn't realize I would die and be taken away!" the boy cried.

"It is highly unlikely that you will fade away from each other. When you have been as close as you two have been, it is very difficult to separate again. The bough usually breaks first. By that I mean the one remaining in the physical usually dies soon after, ending the physical separation. With other beings though, as I have said, they walk on alone, on both levels. Their unions were only temporary to fill temporary needs, and they will create other unions of importance wherever they may go. They will visit the physical plane now and again, to check on their loved ones progress. They may even establish rudimentary forms of communication, passing back and forth information or assisting them at times of difficulty. But they remain separate, for they are separate souls. And this communication lessens in time with them, as other things take their place. It is the same amongst the living who decide to go on and restructure their lives, for they think that their loved ones are gone and beyond their reach. To them, death is the end of their unions, for they cannot see beyond the boundaries of their own minds to open their hearts to the truth. Their loved ones still exist. But they choose not to continue with these relationships. It is partly fear, partly an inability to communicate successfully, and also, it is partly wanting their needs met in the moment. It is too difficult for them to maintain a multidimensional relationship. As you well know, sometimes love is not gratifying. It can be troublesome. But, if it is true, it will last and nothing will deflect you from it. True love weathers all storms and lasts forever. For those who let go, their bonds were not as yours. They have more of a universal bond, which is a bond that everyone shares and is of a lesser degree."

"But you two have the capability and the desire to go beyond that into a true partnership in time. One that is unlimited in love and whose journey knows no end. To maintain your marriage and your commitment to each other, despite the illusion of separation and the changing circumstances. Though the universe may spin around you, you can find the axis solid within each other and your union. That would never change. It would be, shall we say, a marriage for all time, without end."

"When you were married on the earth plane in the third dimension, the words were scripted by man. The oath stated was a limited one. It stated till death do you part. You were unaware at that time, of the changing events and the multidimensional qualities of man. God, who knows no true limits to love or time, did not write those words. Will you limit your love and your union to that oath, or will you take another for the rest of eternity?"

"I will leave you now to reflect on those things which I have told you. The answers to all your questions lie within the truth of your heart. When you know that truth, state it, and it will start you on the path that you have chosen. All comes from within and you have the power to create your own destiny. But remember, whatever is spoken in His name is not to be taken lightly. It becomes an irrevocable trust between you and God, one that will never be broken." With that the guide left the room.

She still lay sleeping. As he watched her, she suddenly sat up and looked around startled. Then she began to cry, silent sobs, with tears streaming down her face. She eased back down on the couch as their dogs surrounded her. Thank God for the dogs, he thought. What would happen if she died, he wondered? I would catch her as she fell, like that first day when we met and we could be together here on the same level of existence. But then, he remembered the girls. What would happen to them if they lost their mother? They might wind up like me, he thought painfully. He shuddered at the possibility of continuing his legacy of anger and abandonment on them, like his parents before him. But there was nothing that he could do, or was there? His head flowed with the overwhelming stream of Victor's words. What if he went back as an infant? The prospect of reliving his life all over again overwhelmed him. And it was just too risky. He wouldn't even be him and he might be born to a stranger. Grandma? That was just ridiculous. He didn't even understand how it might happen, if it even could. It better not happen to those girls, he thought angrily. But what if he were born to her? He would be her child, not her husband. And Victor had said that she would die before him and then they would have to start all over again. They would be separated again for the second time in the same lifetime. And that would mean she would have to sleep with another man.

He became enraged at the thought of her being with another man. The thought of her sharing those things that she had only shared with him drove him to the brink of insanity. He was her husband not anyone else.

Then he felt the truth. The answer was in his heart that he had been looking for. It was really very simple. He was still her husband. Nothing had really changed between them, except for the external circumstances. God had created a universe undivided and all time and space were one.

149

Suddenly he knew what to do. He could never leave her behind, any more than she could leave him. He couldn't abandon the children either. Heaven, or Hell could wait for him. They would be together. They had their children to raise and a marriage to tend to. Things were different, but not over. Then, when the children were safely grown and had their own lives, she was going with him. Like it was supposed to be. It was only natural. This separation had been worse than death, for it was like leaving a part of himself behind. But he would fix that now.

In his agony and in his defiance and in the truth of the love within his heart, he shouted his oath, "I swear to God I will never leave her. I want to take care of her and raise the children with her, as I should have done before. I want to make a difference in their lives. I want to be together as husband and wife forever, in life and in death, no matter what it brings. Death never parted us and never will."

There was no response, just stillness. But he suddenly felt better, for he knew the truth of his own heart. The sound of his voice echoed his oath throughout the canyons of the universe, reaching places unknown. And as he spoke, it was recorded in The Book of All Souls and the Creator of life heard every word.

She had not been in the bedroom since the night he had died there. She was not able to face the physical signs of his death, like the dark blood stains splattered on the wall and on the bed that they had shared. Dealing with his physical absence was hard enough. She could not feel his energy which had been so strongly present in the years that they had been together. She was numb.

The house felt different. It was as if the sweet scent of his soul had suddenly vanished, never to be there again. It changed the very air that she breathed. She felt on the edge of a great abyss that had no bottom and any sudden movement would push her over that edge, following in his footsteps.

So she didn't move. She sat still on the couch, only moving infrequently to refill her bottomless coffee cup and to get more cigarettes. Sometimes, she jumped when the phone rang, always hoping against hope that it was him.

There was nothing anyone could do to help her. Her best friend, Jane, a channel also, knew that she was dying inside. So she counseled her as only she could, to remember who she was and what she believed in. They prayed together for guidance. For Jane had seen upon his death, his return home. She knew that they could be together again in a different way. But she had to awaken her friend to the possibility before it was too late to save her.

Her friend's faith gave her hope. But her grief was too strong and had settled around her, holding her like a fly in a spider's web and she couldn't move beyond it. Fluidity of motion helps and this would have greatly assisted her in clearing her channel, but she was unable to move. Lost in her grief, her energy began to settle into a pool of muddy inertia that threatened to bury her alive. She was stuck in the quicksand of her pain and she was her own worst enemy at that time. Caught in the darkness of his death and the confusion of her own mind, she could not see him. She was still in shock.

Yet, somewhere in the pitch black of her mind, there was a tiny light, which shone like a glistening tear in the ebony sea of her despair. She couldn't believe it was over and that he was gone. They had loved each other more than was humanly possible.

From her heart, she implored the God that she knew so well to bring him back. She called to her husband in her mind, begging him not to leave her behind. She was ready to follow him wherever he had gone. She would die for him.

Then she remembered Matheu. Where was he, she thought? Why wasn't he doing something? She couldn't feel a thing around her. She was half dead herself, and she knew that she was too weak. Some things could not be changed, but she thought Matheu could try to help them in some way.

With a cry that only comes from those that are mortally wounded, she called to her guide. This cry echoed throughout the universe. It was the sound of a broken heart, or of a gentle animal caught in a trap. It was the sound of all men caught in the snare of life, facing their aloneness and their fear of death.

She was too grief stricken to realize that Matheu was already there, sending her gentle energy to keep her from toppling over the edge of the abyss. Had he not been there, she might have already been gone. Ever vigilant, he had never left her, but had stood somewhat back from her, to allow her husband's energy to remain close to her for both their sakes. He did not wish to obstruct the flow between them. But in her pain she could neither see the great guide, nor her husband and was really only slightly aware of her children, who tiptoed silently around the house.

In her pain, she begged the invisible guide to find him, to see if he was all right and to deliver her message of love to him. Then she cried out again in the same shattering way to her old friend Mary Claire, the nun, who had been like a mother to her, asking her to do the same. So she sent the best to him that she knew, in the form of her spirit mother and father, knowing that they would love him as they had loved her. Then, exhausted, she lay back down and waited for a sign of his existence.

He could not bear the sound of her pain. It was a louder explosion within him than the bullet that had killed him. He wanted to shoot himself all over again, in hopes of dying from that place and returning to her on the other side.

Victor returned and suggested that they go to the library as a distraction. So unwillingly, he returned with the guide to further read The Book of All Souls, still watching her helplessly, his heart breaking, as she wept without hope.

He was very angry at God for not helping them. It was at that moment that they came to him. One minute, he could see her clearly in the distance, and the next, there were figures forming in between them that partially blocked his vision of her. He felt very frightened as he sat there watching the figures take shape between them. Victor stood by his side saying nothing.

They were the first people that he had seen since his death, other than his wife and Victor, and for a minute, he wanted to run. He had not wanted to meet any more people. He didn't want to form any other connections, to make this place seem more real than it already was.

Maybe his anger at God had brought them here, he thought. Curiousity got the better of him as he searched their faces. They were an odd looking couple. One was an elderly nun, dressed in a traditional nun's habit, that swept the floor. But she seemed to be wearing sneakers. A nun in sneakers, he thought? I have lost my mind. But her face was warm and motherly, and the minute he looked into her eyes he felt comfortable. She seemed to pose no threat to him. But the other one was unlike any of the others that he had met. He was very tall and forboding. He wore a monk's robe and hood, so you could not clearly see his face. He appeared different than the nun in some way. His energy, which emanated from his being, felt stronger. It was somehow, more electric. The room seemed supercharged in his presence. Yet, there was something familiar about him, but the cowboy could not understand what. Maybe, he thought, this is Judgement Day. He felt the monk's eyes boring a hole through him, deep into the depths of his soul and neither spoke for what seemed like forever, but was really only a short time.

The nun approached him soundlessly and gently sat down beside him. In a motherly voice that soothed him, she introduced herself. "I know who you are my son. It is a pleasure to meet you. I am Mary Claire, and I have been your wife's special friend since she was a girl. I love her dearly. I have tried to be a mother to her over the years and we have grown very close. She is in agony. She has asked me to find you, her beloved husband and to tell you how much she loves you. She blames herself for your death. She is afraid that you do not love her anymore and that you are lost to her forever. I can also see that her fear is untrue, for you are as frightened and as sad as she is. So I have come to help you both in any way that I can." She put her arms around the trembling shoulders of the cowboy, and in that instant, he knew the meaning of motherly love. Turning to the other guide, she scolded him. "Come here," she said to him.

The tall guide slowly approached them and when he did the cowboy's hair literally stood on end. He seemed much more powerful than the other two. Yet, he meekly obeyed the nun. Whoever he is, the boy thought, he is not from here. As he approached, the boy could see into the hood and his face became clearer. There was no expression on it and the only thing that stood out from his angular features were his piercing blue eyes.

153

The eyes penetrated him in such a way that the cowboy wished he could vanish, but he didn't know how.

Then, all of a sudden, the stern face broke into a wry smile, which was like the first glimmer of sunshine after a storm. Then he spoke, "My name is Matheu. Surely you have heard of me. I am for all purposes here, your father-in-law." Mary Claire just laughed.

Then the cowboy realized why he had recognized him. He was obviously someone of a higher energy, for there was a magnetic intensity around him that the boy had never felt before. That intensity had reminded him of someone else. He realized then that it was his wife. He had felt a similar energy around her. Then it hit him. She had been telling him the truth about her guide all along and he hadn't listened to her. He had been afraid to hear it, so he had silenced her.

Spirit was not real to him then. Yet, he was spirit now and here he was, facing the great Matheu, who he had secretly felt was his only competition and whose very mention of his name brought him feelings of resentment and jealousy.

To hear his wife and the girls talk of the guide made him feel as if Matheu could practically walk on water. Upon meeting him, the boy thought silently, perhaps he could. He had told them that he did not believe in guides or even God. They did not exist in the real world and could not protect them as he could. He was flesh and blood and the only protector of his family that they would ever need.

He had told them to get a grip on reality, when he secretly feared that he was real, but couldn't admit it, even to himself, for he could not control an invisible being as he could control other things. So he had brashly denied his existence and banished the subject of the guide from his home, trying to keep them to himself.

But now he was face to face with his wife's formidable protector. The man or whatever he was, that he had secretly called the Hocus Pocus man.

The great guide listened to the boy's thoughts with saitsfaction. He knew this meeting was more important than the boy could ever know, for it validated her work in his eyes. He had always withheld that validation from her, and she had spent her lifetime with him walking an invisible line between the dimensions, torn between both worlds. Honoring spirit and honoring him, yet never being able to completely integrate her extended universal family due to his extreme stubborness. The best of the universe had come to his home to help him, but he had denied them. Now, there could be no denial, and it was up to the guide himself to bridge the gap.

Sitting down on the other side of the cowboy, he began to gently speak. "Do you know what a guide truly is JJ?" he asked. The cowboy shook his head. "A guide is someone who unconditionally loves you. There may be those who would call a guide an angel, but that is not accurate. There are greater beings known as angels, but they serve a different purpose in the universe."

"A guide has lived a mortal existence, perhaps many mortal existences, depending on the individual, so a guide has walked in your shoes many times over, experiencing many of the same things you have experienced. Then, in spirit, he has entered into service with God his Creator, to help those that are still in physical form, to love them unconditionally and without judgement, as God loves all his children and to daily guide them to a better and higher quality of life. Now, I have guided your wife and have loved her very much in this way. All people have guides, though most are unaware of their presence. Their guides secretly influence them, despite this unawareness, perhaps by putting positive thoughts in their mind, or by answering their questions by placing revealing circumstances or objects around them. Have you never pondered over a question to find the answer in an unexpected way? That is the mark of a guide. For some, the contact is more direct. You wife has shown a great ability to transcend the dimensions and to maintain that level through *her* daily existence, so I have worked with her on a direct and physical level. To her, I am a physical being, and to me, she is my pride and joy. The pun is intentional."

"Guides come from different levels of existence, depending upon the growth and the needs of the individual they are guiding.

I am from the eighteenth dimension in the Causal Plane, where great responsibilty lies for creating your own reality."

"Guides are often mistaken for angels, who are very different. Not all angels have lived a physical incarnation, but have chosen to remain as spiritual beings evolving in growth continuously in spirit form. There are no true guardian angels. That is just a man made expression, for angels serve a broader universal purpose and all angels are all guardians of mankind. They serve the Creator directly and oversee mankind as a whole, only interfering on an individual basis when it is necessary for a higher purpose. Being a guide is very much like being a parent as it is done on a personal, rather than on a universal level."

"I have acted as your wife's father, helping to raise her and to guide her to the beautiful woman she has become, whom you love. But guides are no different from mortal men in that they too have feelings. It is true that as one progresses, the feelings become more manageable and less destructive, but guides are quite capable of feeling anger and joy and sadness, as you do, for feelings are a necessary part of growth in that they promote the individual soul to a higher understanding. Even God himself has feelings, in watching his individual children grow through their experiences and in viewing mankind as a whole."

"In watching you over the years with your wife, who I consider to be my daughter, I have experienced many feelings. You have been a source of growth to me and for that I thank you. I have felt frustration at times and also happiness at your mutual devotion. But I want you to know, that I have never once judged you or stopped loving you, no matter what the circumstances of your behavior. I have come here to offer you my hand in friendship. Even though at times your behavior has angered me, I, like she who loves you and like the God who created you, will never abandon you or stop loving you."

The guide extended his hand to the boy and then his whole arm, and they embraced like father and son. A bridge was built that day between Heaven and Earth, for the high guide and the boy of the mountains had come together to form a union based on a common bond, which was the love of a girl.

But she was not able to join them in the celebration, being completely unaware that they were together. Turning to Matheu, the boy said, "I don't know what to do. I am afraid I have lost her for good." And he cried in the arms of the guide, who tried to comfort him as he had comforted her before.

Matheu said, "If your love is true, then you cannot lose each other. If you wish to continue your marriage, then you must take responsibilty for it. It has not ended, but the circumstances around it have changed. First, you must start communicating with each other. You yourself, must take the first step before she sinks too deeply in her pain. She is very weak and has been immobilized by your death. This will renew your bond with her. You see, she too, is afraid that you are forever gone to her and she blames herself. There is only one thing that can separate you and that is fear. It lowers the vibration and one becomes earthbound. Your love will unite you. She is sinking fast, so you must act quickly. She may not hear you at first, but she will feel you physically and then we can work on teaching you the dynamics of interdimensional communication and travel, so that you can be with her as I have been. She is a natural channel and a quick learner, and once she knows that you are there, she will easily adjust her frequency to be able to hear you."

"But I am not a guide. I don't know how to do it," the boy said.

"You are not a guide, this is true, but in your love for her you are stronger than you know and so is she. I and the God that created you, will not allow you to fall in fear, when you have come so far in love. Trust Him and in trusting Him, trust me."

"Now, come with me." And they both stood up and taking the boy's arm, the guide led him into the distance of her living room. Standing together, they were inches from her. She seemed like a dream to him that was beyond his reach. "Believe in it and it will be so. Close your eyes and will yourself to her."

The cowboy was afraid to fail, but something beyond his mind drove him forward. It was his heart. He closed his eyes and thought of holding her close to him with all his might. All of a sudden, he felt a peculiar sensation in his body. It was as if he were moving without moving his feet, and in an instant he was within her. He could feel her all around him, like a moist warm and wet blanket surrounding him, filling him with the sweetness of her scent and the strength of her gentle energy. For an instant, he felt lost in her incredible pain and despair, and in that moment, he knew the depth of her love for him, for they were one being, sharing the same soul, as mind, body and spirit came together in a single heatbeat. Then, all of a sudden, it was over, and he found himself beyond her again. It was an incredible feeling, this feeling of oneness, and he was elated at this highest of unions, which even surpassed the mortal feeling of making love. He felt more married than ever before. He searched her face for a sign of recognition.

She sat up with a start. There was an energy around her and it was very heavy. It was not like Matheu's energy, which was light and intense, or like any of the other guides that she had felt before. It felt almost human in its weight. She felt the warmth and the wetness engulf her, as if she were wrapped in it. Then it penetrated her and she realized who it was. Crying out his name, she allowed his energy to move into her being, welcoming it, till she thought she would burst with fulfillment. The half human, half spirit energy left her after a few minutes, and she cried out his name again. "Cowboy, I know you are here. I love you. Please don't go away and leave me again." The dogs went crazy, not quite recognizing who was there, but knowing someone was.

The guide stood by the weeping children smiling broadly. It was going to take time, but the barrier had been broken and the first communication had been established that would aid them in continuing their union and in fulfilling the higher purpose of that union. But the most important thing was the cowboy was home and they both knew it.

While the real world was busy declaring him officially dead, she knew that he was still alive somewhere and with that came the hope that she would see him again.

She was not of this world. On the surface, she appeared to be the same as everyone else. But her experiences had made her different, for she knew what lay beyond the illusion of the physical reality, having been raised by Matheu and the other guides. But this was her first personal experience with death. It was a test of her faith and what she had been taught by them.

She knew she had to go into the bedroom. His energy would be stronger in there than anywhere else, for that was their private sanctuary together. She knew that was the best way to break through the barrier of her pain to communicate with him. She had to go find him, as he had found her in the living room. It takes two in partnership to truly dance and it was her turn to lead.

On the other side of time he sat alone, watching and willing her with all of his strength, to break through the fear of the blood.

She got up and went cautiously to the door of their bedroom. All the treasures of their life lay within it. She opened the door and entered the chapel of his death. There was an intense energy in the room. It was a mix of love, fear, anger and pain, and at first, she was overhelmed by it. The room smelled of him. She focused her eyes on the corner of the room, away from the blood. She breathed deeply, swallowing as much of him as she could. His clothes lay in the corner on the floor, crumpled, as he had so carelessly left them, with his riding boots and spurs tossed nearby. His hat, as usual, was carefully hung on a peg. She turned her head and saw the ocean of his body, red and dried on the mattress where it had flowed and splattered on the wall behind it. Instead of backing away from it, she did what she had always been taught by Matheu, which was to move forward into your fear. So she walked to it and putting out her hand, she caressed it as if she were caressing him. Then she lay down in the pool of blood itself, hoping to drown herself in what had once been him, calling out his name in her heart.

All of a sudden she felt him there, but this time it was different, for as that hot and heavy energy surrounded her and penetrated her being, she heard him calling her name.

He sounded crystal clear, almost amplified and he spoke forcefully and quickly, as if he were afraid that the communication would fade away and the magic of the moment would be lost to them.

"Sweetheart, I love you and I'm sorry for what happened. It was not your fault or the children's fault. I didn't mean to shoot myself. It was a mistake and I am trying to come back home. There was a big explosion and a blinding light in my head and I died instantly. There was no pain. I'm okay. I woke up by a campfire. An old man brought me a blanket and took me to a place to figure things out and is helping me. I met your guides and your were right about them. They are helping me too. Don't quit on me and the kids. You have to eat something and take care of yourself. Keep raising the children, they belong to us, not to your ex-husband. I want to come home more than anything and I am going to find a way. I love you more than you'll ever know."

Then it was over. She felt a little better, for this confirmed that he had survived and was not alone. He still sounded like himself and he wanted to come back home again. He hadn't left her. But that feeling of calmness passed very quickly and she began to panic when she thought of him in another place. Where was he and who was he with and how could he find a way to come home again, she thought? He had been in many bad situations before this, due to his drinking, but he had always been able to come home again. But this had gone way beyond the norm of passing out in a strange place or waking up in jail. He had killed himself and even though it was unintentional, the result was still the same. His body was dead and he could not come home.

In her panic, she was thinking as a wife, not as a channel. She didn't understand the full meaning of what had happened that night. She only knew that there had been a terrible darkness that had threatened them all and had taken his life from him.

But now she also knew that he had escaped the darkness and was safe with the guides. She was very grateful for that. But it was only because she was a channel that she had heard him at all. He was struggling hard to be with her again. She felt it. But what could they do? Her human feelings fought against her higher self for control of her emotions, as she struggled to cope with what had happened. She felt sure he was in a healing place for the first time in his life. She knew the guides would love him as they had loved her. She was happy about that. But inside, she was still a woman who had lost her husband. She wanted him back. She was afraid that the price of his healing might cost them their love.

Reality hit very hard. She had to make funeral arrangements. She did not want to let his body go, but she had no other choice. They had spoken of it beforehand, in the event that one or the other would die, so she did her best for him in the manner that they had agreed on. She painfully followed his instructions, for she felt him pushing her with his massive energy. He was becoming very strong for her. She felt him intensely, continuously guiding her from the other side of time, feeding her heart, murmuring sweet nothings that only her ears could hear, sustaining her soul and providing the strength to her spirit that was broken without him. For him and because of him, she got through it. He alone carried her with his energy. And the guides carried him.

It was to be a cowboy's funeral, simple but beautiful, with many red flowers on an oaken bier. He would wear his riding clothes and the theme from Lonesome Dove would eulogize him with its melody. No one would be invited, except for her and their children. He did not want anyone from his past there. He would not have those that had abandoned him in life, pretend they cared for him in death. In life, it had always been them against the rest of the world and it still was, even in death.

She began to feel him physically more and more, especially at night when she lay very quiet in their bed. He still bore the partial energy of a human male and she could feel his warmth and his heaviness upon her, unlike the pure spirit energy of the guides. She allowed him to penetrate her being, welcoming him into her body and her soul, until she knew for a fact that spirits do make love. Because of the weight of his energy, she knew he had not yet completed his transition to spirit and she was grateful that he remained somewhat like his old self. He was still him, though invisible. He was clinging to his mortality and to her and she clung back with everything she had. They would not willingly be separated. Neither one wanted to let go of the other and what they had together.

She knew Matheu was with him, helping and teaching him. Matheu loved her like no one ever had and she had never been able to share that love with the cowboy directly, because he wouldn't allow it. But now he could feel it for himself and she knew that no one could love and help him like Matheu.

It was hard to hear him at first. It was much easier to feel him. Even the children could feel him. But they both kept trying all the time, him yelling his words, her straining to hear them clearly. At first the words seemed unclear and garbled as they broke through the barrier of her mind, but they were getting better at it. At times he spoke of coming back as her child in desperation, as if he wanted her to go right out and get pregnant, so desperate was he to come home in the physical sense.

At one point she was ready to make an appointment with a fertility doctor, but the guides held her back." Wait," they said, "There is a better way coming, but you have to work your way there." Life is always a process, getting from one place to the other, so she waited and trusted, with the communication coming in bits and pieces that she struggled to put together like a puzzle, while still feeling the incredible full force of his arms physically reaching out to her.

The funeral was difficult for them both. He was dressed in the uniform of his life and looked like a character out of a western, with his vest and his suspenders, his gold pocket watch placed just right, and his bandana casually tied around his neck. He seemed to be sleeping, as if he had just tied up his horse somewhere and had laid down to take a nap. They had carefully repaired the damage to his head done by his gun. He was very handsome.

She moved a chair to sit beside him where he lay, covered by a blanket of flowers. She stroked his face and his arms and his legs, hoping to bring some warmth to the Arctic wasteland of his skin. But he lay cold and frozen to her touch, and no matter how hard she tried, she could not revive him. She continued to stroke him, until her hands were as cold as his and she too smelled like death. She lifted his lifeless shoulders from his bed and held him close, crooning to him as she kissed him, hoping that he could feel it. She lay her head upon his chest, burrowing her face in his breast, which held the heart that she loved. On his breast, she placed a picture of them together with the girls and a crystal that she had worn, which bore her energy. His death was her death as she lay the silver crucifix given to her by her mother in his hands. He received the last rites of her faith.

On the other side of time, he watched it all. He felt every kiss and every stroke of her hand in his immortal soul. Through her efforts that day, he felt life again, for he felt it through her. It was as if every caress gave him a part of her which he could never lose. He could not speak that day, so moved was he, but was only able to receive the majesty of her feelings for him.

With his cremation, the threads broke and he was a free man. She felt it and she wept, for now she knew he was truly spirit and not a man. He had made the transition and she began to feel a lightness in his energy that had not been there before. His vibration became higher and his essence became less dense. He was still there physically, but he had completed the metamorphosis.

Now she knew many people in the physical world, but she secluded herself from them, not wanting anyone to break the spell that lay between them. He did the same thing on the other side of time, for he did not want to build a separate life there. They both worked feverishly on their communication, day and night, to build a solid bridge between them and the dimensions. They did not want to lose touch with each other at any time. They wanted it to be as it had been before. The harder they worked at it, the stronger it became. The guides continued teaching them both daily, knowing this seclusion was a necessary part of their training. They also knew as their foundation became more solid, they could expand it into the world.

He started to sing to her in the mornings, at that vulnerable time when she was just waking up and opening her eyes to find him gone. She will never forget the morning when she was awoken by the sound of him singing The Beatle's song, In My Life. She hadn't heard it for years and he himself had never been especially fond of the Beatle's music, being more of an Elvis man. But he had found a way to get his message through to her,

163

when he sang that out of all the places and the people he had loved, he loved her more.

He sang this song and many other songs, always unexpectedly, like a cosmic radio station broadcasting only to her.

Despite their limited energy, they worked nonstop on mastering their communication. He worked hard at directing his physical energy towards her being, until he learned to hold her as when he had a physical body. She worked as hard at elevating her being to receive that love and to return it.

Late at night, when all energy had been spent and she had fallen asleep and he himself lay watching her, he swore to remain alive for her, as if he were still physically there.

Because of their determination to stay together, the dimensions were becoming one. Had they thought about it, they would have realized that their legacy came from a higher place and that it was a miracle.

In their world which denied all illusion, he proposed to her once more and she accepted. They each then took an oath, to stay together in God's name, in an eternal union and a partnership for all time. This oath was forever recorded in The Book of All Souls.

They would grow together, finishing their tasks and raising their children, until she would come to join him more fully after her death to progress together for all time.

They then lived this oath, following in the footsteps of their soul parents before them, Astarte and Mahade, on the path of the heart.

Fear had split the universe and the family of all souls, but unconditional love was bringing them together again. Those barriers, that extended beyond the physical into the spirit plane, making it impossible for those who had physically died to continue their relationships uninterrupted with the living, if they so chose, were slowly changing.

They worked hard at unifying themselves in both thought and deed, slowly becoming of one heart and one mind, in one time and one place. Heaven was within them, for they were becoming one with the heart of God.

The harder they worked at uniting, the more they grew, for as everyone knows, unconditional love and true commitment is the essence of all spiritual growth.

They had much work to do to achieve this. Self examination and healing were required for him to learn to love without fear and anger. She had to learn to receive that love without fear of punishment from him. They were each other's healing and their continuing relationship became their classroom.

She could not explain to the rest of the third dimensional world what was happening, because it was beyond their understanding, with the exception of those who already knew because they could see for themselves. To the others with limited perceptions, who would tell her to marry again, she would laugh and answer, "I am already married."

He had experienced a separate reality, but had chosen her instead. He was in total focus on healing himself and on rebuilding their lives together in the best way that he could under the circumstances. He was learning to love.

They had the full support of the guides who constantly encouraged them, because of their love and because of the ability of that love to bring the world to a higher place, simply through its existence, for as everyone knows one in the network of life can influence all others.

With the coming of the millenium, there would be a unified faith. Organized religions which pitted man against man, belief system against belief system, would give way to unity of spirit, in unconditional love and unyielding faith, instead of fear and doubt. Man would accept his fellow man in his heart and in doing so would unite with the heart of God.

But while this was happening, the majority still saw only the differences between each other, instead of the common bond which linked all humanity to itself and to its Creator.

The evolutionary process of mankind's growth was beginning to accelerate in the direction of unity, but they were already there. Science was exploring the multidimensionality of man and time travel, interest in quantum physics was rising, but they were already living it.

During those many months of integrating their beings, when others caught up in the illusion would have told them to go on separately, they said no. And their efforts were not ignored by the Creator who had created a universe undivided.

Even though he had limited energy, he was becoming very strong at channeling it in her direction. He had been gifted with an iron will in physical life and he remained the same in the afterlife. He was becoming a master at verbal communication and at directing his energy to her physically, so that she could feel his ethereal body. He said he had the longest arms in the universe.

She was just as stubborn as he was. Through her previous channeling she had been cellularly restructured to receive spirit. Her body had adapted over time. But she was used to channeling a higher frequency, which was that of the guides. She had to learn to adjust her frequency to his. Their guides, who were much more skilled than they were, could easily adjust their own vibratory rate to be included in on the conversation. At times it was like a party line, with everyone speaking at once.

No greater teachers existed than Matheu and Victor. They taught him to love himself and through that came the ability to sustain her. They taught him the art of manifesting, so that *he* could create his own physical reality in which to exist with her, for it was up to him to build their world. Then they taught her to inhabit it with him, leaving her own physical world behind.

In the living world, there were many channels who acknowledged what they were doing. But out of the many that they knew, there was only one who was a part of their hearts.

Jane had always stuck by them, loving them both unconditionally, without the harsh judgement of the rest of the world. She honored the soul and not the flesh, which made her different from most.

Her brilliant green eyes sparkled with light and she was a great beauty, both within and without. She was a dancer at heart, but the strength of her soul had lifted her beyond the limited ground of the physical world and she danced to tunes not only of the earth, but of the higher dimensions. Her senses were eagle sharp and she could see far beyond the world in which they lived. She had always loved Joy and Joy had always loved her, for they were equals in a world where few could understand them. And they had always stood by each other, viewing the world in a different way from the rest, seeing above and beyond the obvious into the certainty and into what was truly happening, instead of what only seemed to be happening. They chose to live the truth, instead of the illusion, true to the God that had created them. She became their greatest support on earth, friend to them in the living world, only equaled by the guides in Heaven.

Whenever Joy weakened, she would always be there for her, reminding her of the truth and helping her to find her inner strength. She was their earthly acknowledgement in a world where few acknowledge each other, even under ordinary circumstances.

She would always know, even before Joy could tell her, what was going on, for she had a great gift and was a true visionary of her time.

Their two children, Jodie and Jennifer, also supported them, for they were both naturally gifted with the divine sight of their mother. They could feel him at times and acknowledged him as a living parent, for their young hearts were greater than most adults. As lovely as they were on the outside, this was but a small reflection of their greater depth within. They had been blessed with incredible abilities and with a formidible determination to use those abilities to make a better world. They were the best of their forthcoming generation and much loved by all.

Those three were a living link between the worlds and some of Heaven's brightest stars on earth.

Even with support, it was still up to them to do the work. To her he was no longer just the best husband in the world, but in the entire universe, and to him, she was the universe.

Many months had passed since his physical death. This time had been spent by both of them on intense self examination, on rebuilding their relationship at a higher level, and on creating their own reality in which to live. Now, he was ready to build them a home, away from the room that the guides had provided for him during his initial healing.

He was becoming stronger every day and as everyone knows, what is growing in light and love cannot be held back, but must be allowed to venture forth to reach its full potential.

Just as a parent must release their child to experience their own life, so did Victor and Matheu set the cowboy free to live with his wife on their own.

In the physical world, people build houses with solid materials, using their hands and their bodies to construct an environment of their own choosing. In the non physical world of energy, people build their own personal environments through the manifestation power of their minds. He knew exactly what he wanted, so he set out to build the perfect home for them to live in together. One that adjoined their worlds and complimented them both.

In the highest dimensions of the light, one might be comfortable with having no structure at all, just being one with the light and maintaining the true essence of the soul, but he wanted to remain as true to her needs as he had when he left her, for she was still stuck in the physical world.

Because of the teachings of Victor and Matheu and because of the strength of his own ability, he became an expert at creating his own reality. He was driven by his need to provide a sense of security for her. So with his mind and with his heart, he pushed the elements of energy into the mortar of his love for her, building them the home of their dreams.

It was a log cabin. He willed each log and each peg into place. It was a haven for her to come to, and also to look forward to living in more permanently, after her physical death, when she joined him on the other side of time, as they waited for their children.

He placed that log cabin in a lush valley, surrounded by formidable mountains, which were very similiar to the mountains that surrounded his earthly home with her. He called it Joy's Valley, at the base of the Forever Mountains.

The cabin was reminiscent of earthly times long past, when men and women lived together in sweet peace, creating their own lives with their bare hands, in touch with themselves, before the demon of technology had stripped them of their truths.

It was a two room cabin, with a small living room that contained a table and chairs, two rockers and a fireplace. Their family pictures were the centerpiece of the mantle. He cared for those objects devotedly, always placing a rose near them with the power of his mind. They mirrored each other almost naturally, for she had her own altar, in their third dimensional home, at which she did the same.

Surrounding the fireplace were the two rockers, one for him and one for her, and he would sit rocking furiously, back and forth, impatiently waiting for her to elevate her energy to join him. There, she would sit with him for hours in trance, sometimes talking incessantly, but sometimes not. Then she would just quietly enjoy feeling the essence of him and being with him under the same roof. Sometimes, she wound up in his rocker on his lap, and he would rock her like a child, telling her stories of when they would be together again, waiting for their children and their grandchildren to join them, before continuing their multidimensional journey.

He had thought of every detail in his creation. The small bedroom had a magnificent brass bed that shone like gold, with a soft feather mattress. Here they would lay sharing secrets until her energy evaporated, and she fell back down with a thud to her own empty bed in the third dimension, knowing that he was still watching her, but she was too tired to feel it.

This was the home they shared in the lowest quadrant of the sixth dimension, above the astral plane and below the rising paths of full spiritual integration. It was in the same place and in the same time, as the home for her physical body in the third dimension, for all time and space are one, and if one had a camera that took multidimensional pictures, it would have appeared as a layer of celluloid transparency, which lay on top of her physical reality and the more solid physical forms. His Forever Mountains and her Superstition Mountains, totally surrounded their joint reality of a home, providing a surreal sense of privacy and protection for them.

In trance, she could experience living in the home he had built for her through her ethereal body, even though her physical body remained in her own third dimensional home. It was the same for him, for he was spirit leading a multidimensional life. He took all of his energy, which he had once poured into drinking and destruction and was turning a negative force into a positive one, by creating a life together for them in the best way that he could. He was healing, and becoming the man that he always wanted to be. Because of this, she was able to go on, raising her children in both faith and love. He gave her not only unconditional love, but the courage to continue her life.

He loved to time travel, surfing the waves of time to eras long past, when they had been together bearing other names and forms. His strong arms would hold her and she would lean into his energy as the current guided them. They traveled through many periods of time together and sometimes the stories ended happily, and sometimes not, but their souls always led them safely back to the beginning to start anew all over again.

Sometimes the guides would visit and they would sit sharing stories, much like when you would have company in the physical world.

It was the best that it could be under the circumstances, but at times, they would both need to replenish their energy, for she was also tending to her earthly chores with his help. Both of them were living in a time warp, in two worlds which overlapped and both of them would need to rest, for it took a great deal of energy.

Sometimes late at night, when her physical body was exhausted, it grounded her spirit and she was forced to rest alone. When this occured she could barely feel him. He also would become depleted in his own dimension. At those times it was difficult for them both. Their energies had been spent and they had to restore themselves to be together again in the full sense of the word. Though they were grateful for what they had, they wanted more. At those times she would cry herself to sleep, for her physical body was in the way of her being with him all the time. He would suffer also, for he did not have a true physical body to comfort her with and his energy had run too low to break the barrier.

Sometimes he would rise earlier than her and prepare suprises for when she joined him. At those times, she never knew what to expect.

He spent time secretly researching her childhood and would bring to her special gifts that she had almost forgotten about over the years.

She had always loved animals and had many dogs growing up on her Pennsylvania farm. As he had Sheba, she also had a dog that was much loved by her, long before she had ever met him. The dog was called Blackie.

The dog had been a starving stray in the streets of Philadelphia, when she brought him home to her farm as a young college student. He had been with her for eighteen years. He was a part of her that had extended from youth into adulthood and into the lives of her own children and though she had never mentioned him to her husband, for it was before his time, he was a part of her heart. As everyone knows, animals love deeply, for they are totally dependent on unconditional love to survive. Only Matheu knew of this dog, for he was there at his death.

One morning she awoke to find Blackie standing by her husband, furiously wagging his tail at the sight of her. With Matheu's help, the cowboy had found the giant black dog and called him forth from the animal dimension, where animals live in tranquility after their physical death. The black dog had come because he loved her and her gentle ways.

The cowboy then began building a ranch for her in the Forever Mountains, where he called forth many of her dogs and horses. That home became a living memorial to her heart over time. She did much the same for him, for their home was exactly the way it had been when he had physically left it, his prized possessions and his animals there waiting for him, as if he were still alive. In every way they could, they honored each other.

He asked that she keep his ashes, so they could eventually be buried together in the same place for all time. So she became the keeper of his body, as he was of her heart and her soul.

He had the benefit of being at a distance, which gave him a greater perspective on the third dimensional physical world. Because of this, he became adept at what had always amused

171

him. He was as good at reading the future, as he was at reading the past, and would warn her of pending problems before they even happened. He was like a look out scout for his family and when a problem was imminent, he would intervene on her behalf by coaching her beforehand, or by physically changing the events as they were happening. He was like a magician and always monitored the big picture of their lives.

At times, the children were annoyed by this, for he seemed to know what they were doing as they were doing it and he would interfere if he didn't approve of their actions. The children did not want to be saved from themselves, yet, he had an uncanny way of rescuing them from the brink of their more daring escapades in the nick of time, much to their chagrin. He was even worse than Matheu, for he watched their every move. The cowboy had not been easy to fool when he was still alive, but now he was impossible to fool. For them, it was like having a giant eyeball in the sky following them around.

But they knew how much their mother worried about them and that he was trying not only to take care of them, but to assure her of their safety, so she would not suffer another great loss. So they learned to accept it with humor and sometimes, were even grateful that he was always there for them, when they got into situations that were over their heads, as all children sometimes do. They finally realized how much he cared by the way he protected them.

He learned to move objects around the house by amassing his physical energy and applying it to get their attention. He would constantly blink the lights in greeting to them. He was determined that no barriers in time or space would prevent him from taking care of his family.

And God help anyone that threatened or disturbed his gentle wife, for he would slap them on the back and create a terrible disturbance in their home late at night, until they got the message to leave her alone. As he was in life, so he was in death, her fierce protector and constant companion.

He began to work very hard at making a physical appearance, for they both longed to stand face to face, that they might see the light in each other's eyes. This was very hard for him to do in combination with what he was already doing, for his energy was limited and though he was getting incredibly strong, most of his power was spent on maintaining their lives together. To make a physical appearance, one must gather all their energy at one time to become dense enough to be physically seen by the naked eye.

But he was very busy healing himself and becoming the family man that he had always wanted to be, so his energy was scarce. But there were a few times when he would tell her that he was going to rest to gather enough for a physical appearance.

At those times she would wait quietly until the glistening gold of his soul would sparkle like stardust in her room. The dogs, including Sheba, would go crazy, fighting this translucent, but visible foe, who they did not recognize to be their master, because his energy felt very different to them from when he was physically alive. They would jump up from their sleep, teeth baring, ferociously growling like jungle animals, clawing at him, but never getting a bite, for he was made of light, not of flesh and blood and he would laugh at their antics and was proud of their protection of her.

But then she could finally see him and the light of his eyes. Their house in the mountains, which was once filled with the dark terror of his drinking, now became filled with the light of his soul and the love of his heart and she never felt alone again, for she knew that he would never leave her.

It was a magical time in the universe, for the chasm between the dimensions was being filled with faith and the worlds were beginning to come full circle through love.

If she did not feel his strength around her, her fragile being felt broken and if he did not feel her loving energy soothing him, he felt as if he were empty and lost in the darkness of himself. Nothing could take the place of each other. Though there were pleasures to be found on both sides, they were empty and lesser pleasures than what they had found through each other, for they defined and completed each other's beings. Their hearts, as their soul parents before them, were broken without each other.

They were almost becoming more of a couple than they had been before when he was still physically alive, for they were totally focused on each other. They had to work harder at maintaining their relationship than most ordinary couples do, who wind up taking each other for granted. They could not take that chance.

When their energy was the strongest, they would physically love, feeling the security of each other's arms, as heaven and earth came together in the fullness of their beings. At those times, they were almost like one soul, instead of two. But when all their energy had been spent and their beings were running low on fuel, they would have to separate again, the minutes seeming like endless hours, until their energies rebuilt themselves.

At those times of exhaustion, when they unwillingly faded from each other's arms into rest, it was traumatic for them both. They clung to each other with all of their strength, until their strength was gone and they were forced to let go to replenish their energy once more.

It is difficult to say who took those times the hardest. The mortal girl with the invisible husband, or the spirit boy, who wanted to be mortal again, with the human wife with the human needs. They needed to be together all of the time, not just most of the time.

One day, when they had spent all of their energy in being together, they finally began to tire once again. That night their energy faded, much as the brilliance of the day fades into the dimness of the dusk and finally the darkness of the night. They were especially sad and alone that night, for it seemed the closer they became, the harder it was for them to let go for even brief moments of time.

She cried that night and couldn't stop crying. Over and over in her mind, she tormented herself to the point of near hysteria. In his bed, the cowboy lay agonizingly watching her, unable to help, for he too was totally spent. All he could do was rebuild his own energy, until he could hold her once again.

The universe is like a living creature. It holds man in its womb, much as a parent cradles a child. Its eyes, which see everything, incorporate those visions into its heart. That huge beast of a being, who had watched them endlessly toil for their

174

love and to maintain their vows, took pity on them, for blind faith does not go unrewarded.

That night Matheu came to her, and standing by her bed, looked down at the girl, and quietly said, "The way is of the Magi." Those words seemed familiar to her, but so tired and upset was she that she could not respond, but finally fell into a troubled sleep with the great guide standing beside her as a sentinel, bringing her some small comfort with his presence.

When she finally slept, the cowboy too, was able to take his rest, knowing that she was calm once again. The next morning the storm had passed and they both awoke feeling full of energy and refreshed, so they were able to enjoy each other's company again.

But Matheu's words stuck in her mind, for it seemed as if she had forgotten something.

Many days passed, smooth and uninterrupted, with them being together, but then that same time came again when they were both exhausted and they were forced to separately rest.

That night she paced restlessly, unable to sleep, as if she were trying to remember something. He sat watching her on the other side of time, frustrated by his inability to help her resolve what she was looking for.

Then, from the recesses of her mind, she heard a sweet voice singing a song. It was barely audible and sounded almost like that of a child. It was her old friend Twinkles, who was a cherub. The song was easily recognizable and flitted gently throughout her being, as he sang, "Silent night, holy night, all is calm, all is bright." It was at that moment that she found the answer she was seeking.

They had done everything that they could to stay together. They had worked day and night to build their communication. They had created a wonderful world of their own to live in together. Their guides had helped them with their superior knowledge. Her best friend and other channels had supported them in their quest. Even their own children had acknowledged them in the physical world. Through it all, they had maintained their marriage, despite his death. It was the best that it could be under the circumstances and they were grateful, for death had not parted them.

But there was something missing and that was a deeper magic. She could not fully join him until her own life was over and that meant separating from her children. They did not want to wait for death, for they sought life instead and longed to be together in the present, all of the time, as they used to be before. When they were tired late at night, when all of their chores were done and their children sleeping, they wanted to rest together in each other's arms. They needed it now, not in some distant hereafter.

Their faith had been great, but there was a deeper faith that went beyond the powers of humankind, that went beyond the generosity of the guides and the angels who had intervened on their behalf. She remembered the voice that had sounded like bells ringing its words, that spoke without effort, yet had moved her whole soul. She remembered the compassion of the greatest heart that she had ever known, who would heal the world, if only the world would let Him. And all she had to do was ask Him. She remembered Matheu's words.

And so she knelt and for the first time in a long time, she put aside her mantle as a channel to become a child again. She began to pray, pouring out her story, hoping that He heard her, begging Him to finally bring her husband home.

Silent tears fell down the cowboy's face, so moved was he that he prayed with her, for he wanted the same thing, but did not quite understand how it could happen. It seemed beyond the realm of possibilty, and he didn't know who he was praying to.

For the next several days they were closer than ever. He did his best to calm her, by reminding her of his oath that he would never leave her again. His suicide still stung him, for it was the source of their separation, which was never what he had intended.

They time traveled together, they played with their animals and shared the fullness of their energies, till once again the inevitable happened and they were forced to rest.

Accepting their fate, but not liking it, they both fell asleep and the night cloaked their desires. The next morning, she awoke eagerly and set about calling him. But there was no answer, and call as she might, he did not respond. He did not seem to be there and there was nothing but a strange silence surrounding her. The atmosphere seemed heavier than usual and she could not get through the deadened air. She began to panic, for she knew he would never leave her of his own free will.

In the midst of her panic, as she sat in her chair by the bedroom window trying to force her energy upward, another answered her call.

The image of a man began to form at her feet. He took shape vaguely at first, almost as a hologram, with the light from the window shining through him. Then he seemed to gather more substance, as he knelt there beside her on bended knee, for his transparent form seemed to fill with that light. He looked up at her, his eyes brimming with love and understanding. In his left hand, he held a long staff, which he leaned upon as he spoke with a voice that sounded like bells.

"Do not be afraid, for I have come to help you. You have worked long and hard at your love and I have come here to take over your labor. You need not struggle any more, for by my hand will you come together and nothing will ever separate you again. Let go of the pain, let go of the fear, for you have my word."

He vanished in an instant, leaving as quickly and as quietly as he had come.

She sat there basking in His energy and His words for a long time. The room seemed filled with Him and she felt like a child in the warmth of His love. But she needed to share it with her husband. She did not know what the vision had meant, only that He would help them. Yet, she was not afraid anymore, for she knew no greater help existed.

She tried to reach her husband again, but still, there was only silence. The voice of her guide told her to wait patiently. So wait she did, and the minutes of the morning stretched like weeks into the afternoon. Finally, many hours later, she sensed her husband's energy returning to her and she heard his voice calling to her in an excited tone.

All the words were rushing out from him at once, so at first, it was difficult sorting them out, but after a few minutes they settled down into their usual, steady rhythm.

He told her that upon awakening, he had tried to reach her, but had felt closed in and try as he might, he could not get beyond himself. It was as if there were a barrier between the dimensions that he could not penetrate with his energy. He began to get very scared, for he could not reach his guide for help either. Feeling very isolated and trapped in this sudden and unexplicable confinement, he went outside to calm himself and sat down with the animals which always seemed to comfort him.

It was there that he saw a man far away in the distance, that appeared to be walking towards him from the surrounding horizon of the Forever Mountains. He could not see much of anything about him, except that he was holding some sort of long walking stick in his hand, which he leaned upon as he moved. As the man drew closer, the grass seemed to part beneath his feet and the horizon became a moving river alive with fluid motion.

The clothing the man wore was draped around him and flowed as he moved, like a flag unfurling in the wind. He was part of all that surrounded him. His garb appeared crisp and fresh, while at the same time, old and worn. It was as blue as the sky and as white as the clouds and seemed like a reflection of the outer light as well as the inner light, which was coming from the liquid depths of his blue eyes, which were bottomless and like the sea itself.

The cowboy froze. He felt awed by this strange person, who contained in his essence the reflected beauty of all around him. The man had a young face, unlined and untroubled, yet, there was wisdom in the way that he carried himself, as he was both master and innocent at the same time. The cowboy was not frightened, for he felt a sense of safety and peace that he had never felt before. He waited speechlessly, not knowing what to expect, but the visitor smiled and sat down next to him, and laying his staff down on the ground, began to speak.

His voice was strong, yet musical, and within a few minutes, the cowboy forgot that he was talking to a stranger, for he felt as if he were speaking with someone of the same age, who not only knew and understood him better than anyone else, but who also shared his most intimate secrets and feelings about things. There was no distance between them, but an immediate bond. The stranger was different from the guides in that he felt human in his feelings and more like a brother. He seemed very natural and ungodlike, in that his whole essence was filled with the common bond of this shared humanity.

The cowboy felt that finally a friend had come to visit, rather than a teacher and they began sharing together the mysteries of life that only two young men can share.

The cowboy told him his story and what he was trying to do. The young man listened attentively and sympathetically while the cowboy spoke. As the young man responded, his voice filled with the compassion of his heart and he said, "I understand how you feel. There was a time when I walked the earth as you did, and my feelings were no different from the other young mortal men at that time or any other time."

"I wanted to experience the same things in growing up as they did. The look of love from a pretty girl, the sweetness of the wine on my lips, the lightheartedness of youth, while surrounded by the safety of my home and the love and pride of my parents protecting me, as I grew from their child into manhood, experiencing for the first time all the exciting fruits the world has to offer, yet treasuring that familiar feeling of family and friends."

"I am human and a part of the family of man. But those fruits were forbidden to me, for I was different in a way that I did not understand. There were other feelings and a force inside of me that at first, I could not accept, so I fought it. I wanted to be like everyone else. I did not want to be different. But that force kept driving me forward from a deeper space within myself."

"You see, on the surface, I was an ordinary young man with the natural feelings of any other ordinary young man. But deep within my soul, I knew who I really was and because of this, what I had to do. Eventually, I learned to move with that river of faith within me, which was my soul and my Father's destiny for me."

"It was not easy. I faced many doubts and temptations along the way. I was born a child and wanted to love and be loved as I grew. But in moving with that greater river that guided me and was a part of me which I could not ignore, I began to understand a deeper love that did not want for itself, but gave to all others instead."

"I had to give up certain pleasures of the world for the deeper pleasures of the soul. I had to overcome those surface temptations that would have taken me away from who I truly was. I had to let go of my physical life to fill a deeper need and the greater will of my Father."

"I understand your pain and your suffering, for I too have suffered greatly and because of this, I have walked your path with you, perhaps, without your knowledge. My pain was very great and my temptations many, and sometimes, I know very well, that it is hard to conquer the demons of your mind, to find the deeper truths of your soul and who you truly are."

"There were many times when I walked alone with only my faith in God to guide me, fighting those same demons in my mind and the fear in my heart, until I overcame them, to accept myself and the destiny that my Father had chosen for me to bear alone."

"When I finally did this, I found that I could love and be loved without end. Do not think that in experiencing those doubts and temptations as I did, that you have failed God. You have never failed God, because you have truly loved another more than yourself despite them. And through this love you have honored God himself. That is all he asks of any man, that his love reach out beyond himself, so the river of faith and love may flow to all in time. It is because of this unconditional love that you have shared, that you will be given one last choice."

"You may return to the physical world if you so desire. The highest form of this love that we have spoken of is for two souls, separate and individual, to merge together within God's light. This is not a temporary union, but permanent and everlasting, as the light itself, to move together as one for all time. If you so choose, your soul and your essence, will become integrated with that of the one you have loved so deeply for all time and you will never be separate again."

"You may return in physical form, as you both have asked, to complete her lifetime and yours together. Sharing your labors and your lessons united in the same body, for you see, bodies are like houses and can hold more than one being at a time. As a soul enters the being of a babe yet to be born, so may your soul enter her female body and be joined with hers."

"You will find that it is the soul that imprints the personality and the physical form, dictating the lessons and the structure of the lifetime. This would mean that after the transmigration of your soul, her life would change, and it would seem very strange to you both, for as close as you have been, you would still be unused to this closeness. Even though you have moved as one being, this would be very different, for you would truly be one being. There would be no distance between you."

"Mankind has become very isolated in his thoughts and his feelings and has learned to love each other at a distance, thinking it safer. But what is hidden cannot be shared, or truly loved. That is a love based upon fear."

"This is love without fear, completely and totally. You would share her feelings and she would share yours, you would experience her thoughts as your own and she would experience yours in the same way. Her pain would become yours and yours hers, for all time."

"Perhaps, at the beginning, unused to this closeness, your personalities would pull against each other for dominance. But, like a calf born with two heads and one heart, you would learn to move together in unison and over a period of time you would become fully integrated with each other, accepting each other, wanting and feeling the same things, a permanent part of each other's mind, body and soul, until there would be no true distinction between you and you would move through the river of time as one, an inseperable part of each other's being."

"It is a very high path and one that you both have been carefully chosen for at this time. You have been preparing for this since you were born. You know the true meaning of love. It is your destiny and part of that deeper river of who you are."

"This would not happen overnight, for her body would need to be prepared. Over time, it would be cellularly restructured to hold your energy along with her own, as it was restructured so long ago, to channel the higher flow of the many guides that came to her. That was the beginning of her preparation for this path as well."

"As her cells enlarge and change over time, this will become visible to the outside world, for she would bear your physical characteristics and personality traits, as well as her own and they would become more apparent in time. Both the feminine and the masculine energies would be present within her physical form. She is a very feminine energy and you are a very masculine one and each of you would have to adjust to sharing the secrets and the intimate feelings of the other."

"You would share each other's joys and sorrows, complete within yourselves and to your children, you would be both mother and father, nurturer and protector, for she would bear your strength and you would bear her loving heart."

"Then all the world will see the true meaning of unconditional love. There are many who profess to love, but who do not love unconditionally. They remain separate in their own shells, shielding themselves from each other and wanting only for their own satisfaction. They do not get beyond themselves to truly open their own hearts. They would not even consider walking in another's shoes, feeling another's pain and carrying another's burdens, as if they were their own. That is but a shallow reflection of a much deeper love."

"You both are different, as I was different, for you are not afraid to truly love and to be loved. This process has already begun for you both, for this is how you have lived since the beginning of time with each other. In the truest sense, you are already one, for you are the greatest part of her heart as she is of yours, of your own free will. The power to become one has always been in your own hearts. This finalization is the culmination of what you have already achieved on your own. This is your Creator's blessing for your union."

"I myself will deliver your soul to hers and you will be married by my hand for all eternity. This is my gift to you and to the rest of the world, who live in fear of death and separation. It is possible for all mankind, who put aside their fears as you have done, to truly love and be loved, as you have."

"Let it be known that this is my sign and my pledge for the coming millenium. For those that are tormented and plagued by the fear of abandonment, they need not fear any more. All they must do is open their hearts to receive that greater flow. When that happens, I will be there and they will no longer be alone, for we will come together, as you both already have."

"If you so choose in your heart for this final step, it will be done, and it will be a living symbol to the many others that suffer so greatly in their hearts. The world will see with their own eyes, the power of faith and love, and through that rising tide, there will be no more separation or death. Isolation and fear will be abolished and there will be Heaven on Earth, as mankind acknowledges God in his heart and as a part of himself. There will be unity for the first time. No one will be lost, but all will be found in the coming years to be healed by this greater force."

"I know that your greatest fear is that you will become separated once again, but because of this, you never will, for you will be a living part of each other."

"I will never abandon you in this quest, nor will I abandon those who will need me in the coming turbulent times. I am coming back for them, as you are going back for the one that you love and in my presence there will be no more death."

"Speak it with your heart and it will be done by my hand. Through my heart you will become one. I am Jesus of Nazareth, and I give you my word."

The young man left the cowboy as he had come, walking like a simple shepherd back into the mountains to attend to his flock which filled the world.

The cowboy felt drunk with the thought of returning home to share her body. He was filled with an incredible energy of love that he had never known before. His true healing had begun, for he had finally found God and through this discovery he finally knew he was loved and always had been. Thoughts flickered in his mind like fireflies around a campfire, coming full circle

183

within him. Through loving her he had found God and through God he would be able to love her forever.

He felt like an astronaut about to walk on the moon for the first time, so excited was he at the thought of returning home. But most of all, he felt grateful that he had been noticed by a loving God and his living Son, in such a vast universe filled with people, when his own parents had forgotten about him in their own small lives. So like the prodigal son preparing to return home after an arduous journey, he was ready to go. He wanted nothing more than to be an inseparable part of her.

They spoke all day long, wondering what it would be like to share each other's skin. He was very masculine and she was the epitomy of femininity. It would be very much like John Wayne becoming one with Mary Who Had a Little Lamb. They had many unanswered questions about how it would work and what it would feel like for him to be wearing her flowing dresses and for her to crave beer.

Victor and Matheu answered their questions. It had only been done once before in the physical ages ago. There were many barriers to overcome in body and it was much easier to come together as one in spirit. But even in the higher dimensions it was rare. Many that came close had turned aside at the last moment to retain their individuality. It was different than Siamese twins, for those bodies contained two souls temporarily. This was becoming one soul being permanently.

The guides made it clear to them that it was also not a temporary imprinting of certain characteristics that one might feel from a physical organ transplant. Everyone knows that cells retain the imprinting of the individual soul. That is the true formation of the personality and ultimately, the life cycle. The individual soul has its own personality and carries with it the blueprint of the life and the life's lessons, which it imprints on the cellular structure of the individual body.

That is why in a family of many children, who are all born of the same parentage and raised in the same way within the same environment, each will be distinctive from the other. It is not genetics, nor is it environment, but it is the soul that makes the personality, that either blossoms or wilts through the unconditional parental love and understanding, or, the lack of it.

Sometimes in a physical organ transplant, the beneficiary of that organ might experience certain tendencies that have been cellularly imprinted by the donor's soul. But that would diminish in time. This would never fade, but become more pronounced, until a permanent joining was achieved, both cellularly and spiritually for all time. All of him would merge into one with all of her. Neither would ever be the same after this.

They would coalesce to each other, growing together over time. She would say and feel things that were not of her, and so would he, but eventually, they would fully accept and integrate with each other, becoming one.

Because of the physical limitations of the human body, they would have a slightly shorter physical life span than the average, for after cellular reconstruction, her physical body could not contain both energies for as long as it could contain a single one. The intensity of the energy would eventually wear out the physical circuitry. But, her body was very strong and it would be long enough for both to complete their lessons and to raise their children together. Ultimately, it really didn't matter, for in remaining separate she would have died of frustration and he would have been unable to progress properly, for his heart would have always been with her. Neither could completely heal if they remained apart. They needed to be together to be completely whole, as their soul parents before them.

But it would be stressful to her physical body, as it had been when she first began her channeling so long ago and was bearing the transient energies of the guides for periods of time.

His energy would not be transient in her body, but would remain bonded to her for the rest of the lifetime until their death. Then they would die together, released from their physical body, still joined but unconstricted, to the higher dimensions of form and energy. There they would progress together. He knew he would have to experience physical death for the second time to come home again. But he was not afraid.

They were told by the guides that her petite form would become mannish, for his physical energy was much larger than

185

hers. She would bear his anger and his pain and together they would face the many lessons of his lifetime, working them through, as well as her own lessons. But he would become more tolerant over time through her loving heart and her infinite patience, to become a true member of a family, as he had always wanted. Her frailty and her shyness would vanish because of his solid strength within her.

Since they would be sharing the same physical energy, when their mutual body tired, they would rest together in it and she would feel him from within, his vibrancy and his life force tingling and spreading throughout her entire being, as he would feel her gentle warmth caressing and comforting him. It would be a splendid communion.

Later, when they were alone, they laughed together at the thought of him shaving her legs and the possibility of her growing a beard. They remembered the Star Trek movie, The Wrath of Khan, when Mr. Spock at his death, had placed his energy in Dr. Mc Coy's body for safekeeping. It seemed much the same was happening to them.

They worried about each other instead of themselves. He knew how important it was for her to feel beautiful. He worried about her reaction to losing her femininity, as it became blended with his more masculine energy. He worried about her life span and if she were cheating herself and the children to become one with him. He worried about his short temper and his anger and how it would change her. Most of all, he worried about his drinking, and whether those urges might affect her. She had never really drunk before, except for an occasional glass of wine. Would his alcoholism change that? But despite it all, in his heart of hearts, he wanted it more than anything, for he knew that through her, he could learn to love and to be loved, for that was the greatest gift of her.

She worried that it would hurt him to die again, for once seemed painful enough for any individual. She was afraid that he might not like her after he truly got to know her from within, for when they were together in the same being, they would have no secrets from each other. She knew how he hated confinement and she worried that he would feel trapped. She was afraid that he would regret it once it happened, for she would not be good enough or exciting enough. But she wanted it more than anything, for he completed her with his courage, his strength and the loyalty of his love.

That night they shared their secret fears and desires, and she said to him once again, "Out of all the souls I have ever known on both sides of time, I love you more. I want to be with you always, if will have me. I don't want to go on without you. I feel like half a person unless you are there with me." And he said to her, "I've already died a thousand times when our energy fades and we can't be together. Do you remember when I used to go away for days at a time looking for myself? Now, I have been everywhere and I finally know where I belong. I have found myself through loving you and I don't want to go on without you, if you are willing to have me. I love you more than you'll ever know. You know we belong together."

So they accepted and they began to prepare for their permanent union, when their two beings would become one in her physical body, in the eyes of God and through the heart of Jesus of Nazareth.

With their acceptance, it was thus recorded in The Book of All Souls, bringing on the onset of many changes.

Her body began to change on its own. That is the power of the soul to alter the physical. Her cells began to restructure themselves, as she prepared for his homecoming. She never changed her eating habits, but she began to retain food in a different way. She did not get fat, but more mannish and try as she might to contain her figure, no matter what she did, she kept getting bigger. He began a complete spiritual cleansing, for he wanted to be as emotionally pure as possible for the transition.

He had walked through her many times before in brief moments, but had never been able to remain there, as he was always repelled back within himself. Her soul was very strong in its protection of her and would not allow any foreign beings to possess her. But now he learned that he would enter it in a different way, much as the soul of a new born baby enters, spiraling downward through the magnetism of life's current into the fourth dimension, which is the entry point of all souls into the physical. That was the only permanent way to be joined.

She asked him if he were afraid to die again, for she was still afraid of the dying process. Dying seemed very different than death itself. He told her quite gently that dying was not to be feared, but welcomed, for it felt like falling, and that he would catch her as she fell, as he always did. He was not afraid to die, but more afraid to live without her love.

The guides encouraged him to experiment with entering her body and trying to remain there, as an adjustment period for them both, but they could not maintain it for long periods of time. But the more he entered her, the more she stretched to fit him. She began to change in personality and became much more aggressive. Once she chased a would be intimidator physically away from her car. She began to affect him in the opposite way, for he became more gentle towards the outside world. Even her eyes began to lighten.

It was physically uncomfortable for them both at first. It was hard for her to contain his bigger physical energy. Several times after he entered her, she collapsed onto the floor racked with pains in her body, gasping for breath trying to hold him. But the more she grew, the easier it became. While this was happening, her mind wandered back to the very beginning, when she had first met Matheu and learned to hold his greater energy within her. She could see that her whole life had been spent in preparation for this.

He told her that he was counting on her will power not to drink, for he could not be sure that once back in physical form, he would not want it again. Though there were times when she began to crave alcohol, she never took a drink in his honor.

Her best friend, Jane, was getting married. Joy wanted to tell her about their upcoming soul merger, but Jane already knew because her own guide, Virginia, had told her. When the two friends spoke, they decided to be married in a double western wedding ceremony in the Superstition Mountains, with only Joy's two daughters present, who were also like daughters to Jane.

188

Like two little girls they giggled over the phone, planning their joint wedding day in which both brides would wear white, and both grooms, one visible and one not, would wear the garb of the cowboy hero.

The soul merger actually began the day before the wedding ceremony, as the cowboy made his long journey to the altar of her soul, to be married by the hand of Christ. All he knew was that he began falling and couldn't touch bottom. He felt as if something were sucking him down a giant vortex of light. He couldn't feel himself, until he landed safely within her and he was unable to leave her skin.

He was confused and frightened at first, as he heard her thoughts and felt her feelings overwhelm him. He couldn't move and he began to panic. He felt trapped and compressed, as if he was wearing tight clothing that didn't fit. He tried to operate her arms and legs, but she had control and he couldn't get them to move. His being felt awkwardly out of proportion, with her large breasts and her hair heavy on his shoulders.

Like a sudden shock, she felt him within her. She was stretched like a balloon to the breaking point. Then, in synchronicity, they started to move awkwardly together. They were cooperating somewhat like Siamese twins.

That night, Jane arrived with Joseph, her fiance, and they spent the night talking to the cowboy in their friend's body, for he was learning to use the power of his own mind over hers. It was a very different conversation than what they were used to. He gave them a lecture on social drinking.

Later, they got to visit more with their gentle friend, as the struggling began to diminish and they all spent a merry evening together as a foursome in three bodies, never knowing who would be talking at what time.

At rest, as she felt his strength and his masculine force fluttering within her, she began to know what it was like to be truly loved. He felt the same ecstasy, safe within the gentleness of her being and the warmth of her loving heart. For the first time in their lives, they felt complete within each other. They slept together in their own bed for the first time since the night he had died there.

Matheu reminded them that this was just the beginning of their growth and their journey. The next step was becoming one with the heart of God, as they progressed together.

The two children had not been told about what was happening. Her mother wanted them to adjust to the change within her, before she announced their soul union. That night, Jodie, her older daughter, dreamt a strange dream, which she did not understand. She dreamt that the cowboy was putting on her mother's clothes for the wedding day. She didn't know how prophetic that dream was until later, when she saw the difference in her mother and was finally told.

The wedding day dawned perfectly. The western sky shone like a sapphire in the ring of eternity. Jane was the picture of beauty in her bridal gown with her handsome prince beside her.

And standing just behind them, in a simple white dress, was the second bride with the Cinderella soul and her handsome prince within her.

They were both married that day, her best friend beginning love's journey with her husband, by the minister's hand and the cowboy and the channel completing their long journey by becoming one being, through Christ's loving heart.

That night, when the other couple had left to go on their honeymoon and they were sitting alone, just enjoying each other's company and feeling complete within themselves, they were thinking about their happy ending.

All of a sudden, their youngest daughter, Jennifer, who was a fine, aspiring writer and who was blissfully unaware of what had happened, bounded out of her bedroom, waving something that she had just written. She said it had just popped into her mind. It said, "Happy endings are like friends. Sometimes, you can't always have the one you want, but if you have confidence and faith, you can get the one you deserve no matter what happens."

Never had truer words been spoken.

Epilogue, Song of Heaven on Earth

Time never stands still but moves forward, sometimes with heavy footsteps that wake up a sleeping world to a new awareness, sometimes stealthily creeping along lightly on cat's paws, which lulls its children into complacency and a soothing sleep of sameness.

With the millenium, many changes had occured. Like a condemned man, mankind had been forced to admit that it was not alone in the universe. Intergalactic travel began with the coming of other life forms. Coexistence had become possible after many great tragedies. Another World War had narrowly been averted and the network of life had been fully restored. The brotherhood of man was reborn and extended into the universe.

The spirit world became more visible, as mankind moved into the light and finally opened their eyes that all time and space were one. All men became seers and doers and God was no longer a convenient commodity or myth, but a living parent. Through the destruction of what was built in arrogance and fear, came the time of the heart and one universal faith. Christ himself had been reborn through the many, instead of the few or the one.

They were truly one being now and had been for a long time. Their work had expanded, for they had given their lives to becoming one with the heart of God.

The children, who were their pride and joy, had grown even stronger filled with faith and love. They were singing their own lullabys and weaving their own fairy tales, with their own princes beside them. Her best friend and her husband had flourished in their union, perhaps even following in their footsteps in times to come.

The cowboy and the channel could hear each other and see each other from within their own self, and they sang sweet songs of mystery together. When she got sad, he would carry her from within and she did the same for him.

They fell asleep one night and shared a dream. They dreamt of Kentucky skies, an open carriage and dancing on the front porch with the sound of fiddles in the background. They dreamt of a secret and forbidden love, of an aristocrat and a simple slave in the darkened hollows of the Egyptian tombs. They dreamt of a flag unfurled and carrying the banner of Christ, while leading an army. Then they dreamt of a handsome cowboy on a horse named Poco and the lovely girl that always rode beside him on a horse named Bud, all the way to eternity.

When their body cracked that night, much as an egg shell cracks, two souls emerged like two yokes joined together. Like a shooting star, they shot straight to home, to awaken in each other's arms, still one being, but able to love each other again unconstricted, in their home in Joy's Valley, at the base of the Forever Mountains.

Shooting stars can go as high as they want, but from there, they would renew their vows to each other. They would guide their children and their grandchildren, until they were all together again. Then and only then, would they move forward, still together as one, to dimensions and worlds unknown, but soon to be discovered.

About the Author

Joy Jenkins is a Master Channel. Her home is in Arizona with her two children. She travels frequently in her work offering private consultations and group seminars on how to communicate with spirit and how to reach your own personal guides.

She has channeled since the early eighties under her soul name Astarte. She has studied the healing arts and is a Reiki Master. She is a gifted prophetess in many areas, including relationships, health, finance, business, past lives, karma, life and soul path readings. She reads the Akashic Records. She channels loved ones that have passed over, your own personal guides and the Ascended Masters. She has studied the world's religions. She is available for private consultation and to speak to your group on these topics and much more.

The Path of The Heart was written by William and Joy Jenkins after William's death, through communication with Joy. They are currently working on a second book, which is part of a trilogy designed to bring a new level of spiritual awareness to the coming times.

For readings, classes and seminar information
contact Joy Jenkins via her website at:
http://thepathoftheheart.tripod.com or
e-mail her at: thepathoftheheart@yahoo.com or
write to her at
P.O. Box 107
Gilbert, Arizona 85299